The American History Series

SERIES EDITORS

John Hope Franklin, *Duke University*

Abraham S. Eisenstadt, *Brooklyn College*

Arthur S. Link
Princeton University
GENERAL EDITOR FOR HISTORY

Allan M. Winkler
MIAMI UNIVERSITY

Home Front U.S.A.

America during World War II

HARLAN DAVIDSON, INC.
ARLINGTON HEIGHTS, ILLINOIS 60004

Library of Congress Cataloging-in-Publication Data

Winkler, Allan M., 1945–
    Home front U.S.A.

    (The American history series)
    Bibliography: p.
    Includes index.
    1. United States—History—1933–1945. 2. World
War, 1939–1945—United States. I. Title. II. Title:
Home front USA. III. Series: American history series
(Harlan Davidson, Inc.)
E806.W55   1986   973.91   85–25209
ISBN 0-88295-835-6

Cover design: Roger Eggers. Cover illustration: Women riveters
in the Long Beach, California, plant of Douglas Aircraft
Company working on a B-17F heavy bomber, October, 1942.
Office of War Information Photo (National Archives/
Imagefinders, Inc.).

Manufactured in the United States of America
97 96 95 94 93 92 MG 5 6 7 8 9 10

For Henry R. Winkler

FOREWORD

Every generation writes its own history, for the reason that it sees the past in the foreshortened perspective of its own experience. This has certainly been true of the writing of American history. The practical aim of our historiography is to offer us a more certain sense of where we are going by helping us understand the road we took in getting where we are. If the substance and nature of our historical writing is changing, it is precisely because our own generation is redefining its direction, much as the generations that preceded us redefined theirs. We are seeking a newer direction, because we are facing new problems, changing our values and premises, and shaping new institutions to meet new needs. Thus, the vitality of the present inspires the vitality of our writing about our past. Today's scholars are hard at work reconsidering every major field of our history: its politics, diplomacy, economy, society, mores, values, sexuality, and status, ethnic, and race relations. No less significantly, our scholars are using newer modes of investigation to probe the ever-expanding domain of the American past.

Our aim, in this American History Series, is to offer the reader a survey of what scholars are saying about the central themes and issues of American history. To present these themes and issues, we have invited scholars who have made notable contributions to the respective fields in which they are writing. Each volume offers the reader a sufficient factual and narrative account for perceiving the larger dimensions of its particular subject. Addressing their respective themes, our authors have undertaken, moreover, to present the conclusions derived by the principal writers on these themes. Beyond that, the authors present their own conclusions about those aspects of their respective subjects that have been matters of difference and controversy. In effect, they have written not only about where the subject stands in today's historiography but also about where they stand on their subject. Each volume closes with an extensive critical essay on the writings of the major authorities on its particular theme.

The books in this series are designed for use in both basic and advanced courses in American history. Such a series has a particular utility in times such as these, when the traditional format of our American history courses is being altered to accommodate a greater diversity of texts and reading materials. The series offers a number of distinct advantages. It extends and deepens the dimensions of course work in American history. In proceeding beyond the confines of the traditional textbook, it makes clear that the study of our past is, more than the student might otherwise infer, at once complex, sophisticated, and profound. It presents American history as a subject of continuing vitality and fresh investigation. The work of experts in their respective fields, it opens up to the student the rich findings of historical inquiry. It invites the student to join, in major fields of research, the many groups of scholars who are pondering anew the central themes and problems of our past. It challenges the student to participate actively in exploring American history and to collaborate in the creative and rigorous adventure of seeking out its wider reaches.

John Hope Franklin

Abraham S. Eisenstadt

ACKNOWLEDGMENTS

This book has drawn extensively on the work of other scholars as well as on original research, and has benefited from the assistance—professional and personal—of a number of people. I would like to thank Richard Polenberg and James T. Patterson for their penetrating criticisms of the text. I am grateful to John Morton Blum, whose own work informs these pages, who first interested me in World War II, and even more important, who showed me how history could and should be written. I appreciate the good will and encouragement of editor Maureen Gilgore Hewitt, who helped make publication possible. I am grateful, as always, to my wife, Alberta, and to our children, Jenny and David, for providing a loving and encouraging atmosphere, at home and abroad. I would like to thank Barbara Clarke Mossberg for all kinds of assistance—for reading the manuscript and critiquing it carefully, and for being a special friend and colleague in our mutual quests. Finally, I want to thank another scholar—my father, Henry R. Winkler, to whom this book is dedicated—for his professional example and his personal support.

CONTENTS

ONE

The Arsenal of Democracy

Participation in World War II had a profound impact upon American society. Although there was no fighting on the soil of the United States, the war engulfed the nation and became the focus of all U.S. activity between 1942 and 1945. It demanded intense military and diplomatic efforts, at levels never undertaken before, to coordinate strategy and tactics with other members of the Grand Alliance. It also required a monumental productive effort at home to provide the materials necessary for warfare.

The United States became a major force in the war. American entrance into the struggle came late—more than two years after hostilities began—but America had been increasingly committed to the Allied cause even before the Japanese attack on Pearl Harbor in December 1941 elicited a declaration of war. U.S. convoys had already been protecting shipments of military and economic aid for the beleagured overseas democracies, and American factories had been providing required support.

Thus, while formal entrance only ratified a process well underway, active involvement gave the United States a vested interest in the outcome and legitimated the enormous effort that was made.

In making that ultimately successful effort, American society changed. The war brought a resurgence of optimism after the enormous hardships of the 1930s. Ravaged by the Great Depression, the United States remained a troubled nation as that decade came to an end. Military spending gave the country's economic system the boost it needed. The nation began to prosper once more as Americans returned to work to make the weapons of war. Various social groups flourished. "Outsiders," previously denied access to the American dream, now found themselves with better jobs than they had ever held. Women played a major role in home-front production. And blacks and members of other minority groups pressed for and finally received a measure of upgrading when it became clear that their participation would make a significant difference in the outcome.

The basic structure of American society became increasingly complex. As the government girded itself for war, bureaucratic organization became even more extensive than during the New Deal. New executive agencies proliferated, and the power of the presidency expanded. In every area, Americans in the years between 1940 and 1945 confronted shifting social and political issues as they adjusted to new patterns that came to dominate their lives. They embraced changes, even as they clung to the values they had held before: Americans wanted a better America within the framework of the past.

FDR: MOBILIZATION
AND THE PRESIDENT

Mobilization was the first priority as Americans prepared for war. Although the United States had the potential to support the entire Allied effort, resources had to be channeled toward appropriate ends, making enormous organizational adjustments a requirement for the nation to operate on a successful war footing.

Presiding over the massive mobilization—and over the entire war effort—was the man who had helped the nation survive the Great Depression. Franklin D. Roosevelt (popularly known as FDR), president since 1933, played a dominant role in the war. He repeatedly engaged in personal diplomacy in an effort to keep the Allies together, followed domestic developments closely, and kept a watchful eye on all aspects of the struggle. Committed to victory above all else, Roosevelt frequently had to make compromises, particularly on issues that surfaced at home; yet he retained the ebullient spirit—and infectious grin—that had sustained the nation in the past and would continue to sustain it during the war.

Historians have disagreed about the success of Roosevelt's New Deal in promoting economic recovery and even reform, but most have acknowledged his remarkable charismatic qualities. He was—as William E. Leuchtenburg (*Franklin D. Roosevelt and the New Deal, 1932–1940,* 1963), Arthur M. Schlesinger, Jr. (*The Age of Roosevelt: The Coming of the New Deal,* 1958; and *The Age of Roosevelt: The Politics of Upheaval,* 1960), and James MacGregor Burns (*Roosevelt: The Lion and the Fox,* 1956)—all have shown, an extraordinary leader. A member of a wealthy, aristocratic New York family, FDR was nonetheless able to persuade ordinary Americans that he had their interests in mind, and to infuse them with his own boundless optimism and confidence that everything would work out. He struck just the right note in his first inaugural address when he declared, "The only thing we have to fear is fear itself."

A master at using the media, he made people understand that

he cared. Recalling one of Roosevelt's legendary radio-broadcast "fireside chats," Frances Perkins, secretary of labor, once observed: "His face would smile and light up as though he were actually sitting on the front porch or in the parlor with them. People felt this, and it bound them to him in affection."

Roosevelt was a complex and sometimes mystifying man. "I cannot come to grips with him!" lamented a loyal cabinet member, who spoke for all who worked with FDR. Yet, complaints notwithstanding, affection for the president remained undiminished throughout his tenure. "A second-class intellect,—but a first-class temperament!" Justice Oliver Wendell Holmes once remarked. And that temperament helped maintain national morale.

Roosevelt fully understood the importance of his role, a role he enjoyed playing upon as much as he could. He loved visiting the troops in his capacity as commander in chief, and delighted in repeating the response he gave to a soldier in North Africa, who gasped "Oh my god" in astonishment at seeing him. "Just for one more term, son," the president said.

During the war years, Roosevelt governed as he had in the past. He was fond of creating conflicting layers of authority, as evidenced by his establishment of agencies that competed with others already in existence. That pattern allowed him to play off assistants against one another, thereby giving them the chance to work out their disagreements themselves, or enabling the president to step in to mediate the inevitable disputes himself if he chose.

Roosevelt acted, as always, with a masterful sense of timing. He had the ability to wait, indefinitely if necessary, until the time for action was right. He would agree to see subordinates to discuss matters about which he was undecided, only to ramble on genially for the entire meeting. Marriner Eccles, governor of the Federal Reserve Board, once recalled how an important meeting never got started, for his allotted time was taken up watching FDR play with his little dog Fala and then scold the pet for "purging himself on the rug." At first furious, Eccles later realized that he had been a victim of the president's way of avoiding controversial situations until he was ready to act.

Roosevelt applied his executive talents to the prickly problem of industrial mobilization. As war in Europe threatened in the late 1930s, American industry remained sluggish, still caught in the cycle of the depression. When the war broke out in September 1939, and the Axis powers—Germany and Italy—quickly established their dominance on the continent, the president began to worry in earnest, for he recognized how important American production would be to the war effort. In May 1940, he asked Congress to appropriate $1 billion for the production of fifty thousand planes. He soon requested even more money. Well before the Japanese attack on Pearl Harbor Roosevelt declared "We must be the great arsenal of democracy."

Although Roosevelt insisted on "speed and speed now," it took time for the economy to gear up, as the country's difficulties were immense. John Morton Blum was one of the first scholars to examine the thorny problems that had to be overcome in *From the Morgenthau Diaries: Years of War, 1941–1945* (1967). Not until mid-1943 was a rational system of economic controls firmly in place. Conversion to a military footing was a prickly process that required central direction, but that direction arrived only after months, even years, of experimentation. As was so often the case, Roosevelt tried first one agency, then another, until he finally found a combination that could work.

Roosevelt's first attempt at direction came in 1939. He appointed a War Resources Board to examine the needs involved in regulation of the economy. Concerned about antiwar sentiment, however, and wary of excessive planning, FDR withheld his own support. "I do not believe that there is an awful lot of Government action that is needed at the present time," he declared in May 1940.

The German blitzkrieg of the Low Countries and France that year changed his mind. To provide better coordination, Roosevelt resurrected the National Defense Advisory Commission, which had functioned during World War I. Its members represented industry, labor, agriculture, and the consuming public and it had several divisions, each concerned with a different aspect of war mobilization. But the commission proved singularly ineffective, for it had only advisory authority and lacked a responsible head.

Still, before America entered the war, Roosevelt created the Office of Production Management in January 1941. He intended it to stimulate industrial production and to resolve manpower and raw materials problems. Codirected by William Knudsen of General Motors and Sidney Hillman of the Amalgamated Clothing Workers of America, it tried to encourage suppliers to promote military needs over civilian desires, but the agency lacked the statutory authority to back up its requests, ran into trouble stemming from divided leadership, and eventually broke down when military requirements for scarce materials outstripped supply.

The failure of the Office of Production Management led to the creation of the War Production Board (WPB) in January 1942. Roosevelt chose Donald Nelson, who had enjoyed a successful business career with Sears, Roebuck & Co., to head the new agency, and gave it the mandate to "exercise general responsibility" over the economy. With the government now requiring civilian industries to convert to military production, the WPB sought to curtail nonessential civilian activity and to implement a system of preferences and priorities.

The WPB suffered, however, from its decision to allow the Army and Navy to retain responsibility for military procurement. Though they had established purchasing agencies, the WPB lost the ability to impose central direction at a time when such direction was necessary to accommodate all economic demands. As the system threatened to break down, the WPB implemented a new Controlled Materials Plan aimed at coordinating needs and supplies, but the agency never managed to provide the direction sought when it was created. As Bruce Catton argued passionately in *The Warlords of Washington* (1948), an account that has provided an interpretive focus for historians in subsequent years, military and business interests took precedence over national concerns.

Nelson was confronted with additional problems when he acquiesced in Roosevelt's decision to appoint "czars" to deal with the problems of manpower, petroleum, and rubber. Bernard Baruch, who had been responsible for industrial coordination during

World War I, warned him that "you must be the boss and when you say anything . . . it just has to go." Nonetheless, Nelson found his authority diminished, and his own inability to act decisively only compounded his problems.

Roosevelt acted once again in May 1943. When military leaders proved unwilling to work with Nelson any longer, the president created a new agency, the Office of War Mobilization (OWM), to be led by James F. Byrnes. Byrnes, formerly a member of the Supreme Court after service as a senator from South Carolina, had most recently headed the Office of Economic Stabilization where he had had authority to mediate disputes between various wartime agencies. The OWM, superimposed on existing organizations, was given policymaking authority and became a court of final appeal when industrial arguments occurred. Byrnes assumed neither operating functions nor administrative chores. Rather, he successfully used his political savvy to provide needed coordination. Byrnes's job was summed up by a WPB official: "Suppose you and I have a disagreement in arithmetic; you claim that two and two make four, while I claim that two and two makes six. We take it to Jimmy Byrnes for a decision. He's apt to get us both to agree that two and two make five."

Conversion to a war economy was never easy; the government encountered problems in every area. A case in point is the experience with the automobile industry, which was crucial to industrial mobilization. Its assembly lines were needed to make planes and tanks, and it was asked to produce one-fifth of all war material in the United States. But car manufacturers were in no hurry. With the country recovering from the depression, their priority was the huge civilian market and its renewed purchasing power. There were profits to be had. Thus, in 1941 they produced nearly a million more cars than in 1939. The War Production Board, at its first meeting, had to outlaw production of cars and trucks so that manufacture of military items could begin. And even then extensions and exemptions complicated the process until the spring of 1942.

Conversion did, however, begin, and once begun, there was no stopping it. In the summer of 1940, Packard accepted a contract for 9,000 Rolls Royce engines and Chrysler agreed to produce tanks in a plant scheduled to be built north of Detroit. The most dramatic venture, however, was the bomber plant built by Henry Ford in southeastern Michigan. When Ford agreed (near the end of 1940) to construct 1,200 B–24 bombers, he planned a gigantic new factory, to be erected thirty-five miles from Detroit in an area called Willow Run. The plant was to be a mile long, with the main building alone covering sixty-seven acres, and in it the airplanes were to be assembled on a single continuous assembly line. Groundbreaking occurred in April 1941, the first parts were produced late that year, and the first bomber appeared the following year. At a final cost of $65 million, the plant contained over 1,600 pieces of heavy machinery as well as 7,500 jigs and other fixtures. When working at full tilt, it employed over 42,000 people. It was, aviator Charles Lindbergh observed, "a sort of Grand Canyon of the mechanized world."

Other ventures were similarly successful. Early in the war the United States found itself with a serious rubber shortage. Japan's seizure of the Dutch East Indies and Malaya had cut off more than 90 percent of America's crude rubber supply, and though half a million tons had been stockpiled, that amount was only enough for one year of consumption. Production of synthetic rubber would have been the answer, but the process in the United States had been slowed down in the late 1920s by an agreement between Standard Oil of New Jersey and I. G. Farbenindustrie, the German chemical firm, that limited American efforts in the area. That agreement may have helped American business at the time, but it clearly hampered the public interest.

With the war underway and the cartel agreement no longer binding, Americans began to consider two possible processes—grain alcohol and petroleum—that could be used to make rubber. Agricultural interests pushed a bill through Congress in the summer of 1942 that would have favored the alcohol method; petroleum administrator Harold Ickes endorsed the petroleum approach; and in the end FDR vetoed the bill. As the nation embarked upon rubber drives and rationing programs, production of synthetic rubber began. The president appointed William Jeffers rubber director in late 1942, and the government spent $700 million to build fifty-one plants that rubber companies then leased. One West Virginia factory run by the United States Rubber Company covered seventy-seven acres and produced 90,000 tons a year. Capacity increased steadily as the program paid off. By 1944, the nation was producing more than 800,000 tons of rubber a year, approximately 87 percent of the total amount used. Another major problem had been overcome.

The American effort to create an atomic bomb was one more area in which U.S. productive might made a difference. For several decades after the war, historians studying the bomb concentrated on the decision to use atomic weapons in 1945. The process of developing the bomb, however, was crucial to the question of its ultimate use. With the declassification of relevant documents, Martin J. Sherwin (*A World Destroyed: The Atomic Bomb and the Grand Alliance, 1941–1945,* 1975) and others have shown what happened in the years before 1945. In August 1939, physicist Albert Einstein wrote Roosevelt a letter in which he observed that "it is conceivable . . . that extremely powerful bombs of a new type may . . . be constructed," and he hinted that the Germans were interested in the possibility. Roosevelt established a committee to look into the matter, but there was little sense of urgency until actual U.S. involvement in the war. After several bureaucratic reorganizations, and a stronger executive commitment, the task of creating an atomic bomb began. It was known as the Manhattan Project.

The United States devoted a great deal of effort to this top-secret quest, including the construction and use of thirty-seven installations in the United States and Canada. New cities were erected at Oak Ridge, Tennessee, at Hanford, Washington, and at Los Alamos, New Mexico. The Manhattan Project, which cost $2 billion—then a huge sum of money—employed 120,000 people. After producing the first self-sustaining atomic chain reaction in history, American scientists then had to find a way to gather enough of a special form of uranium, or to produce enough plutonium, to mold into a bomb.

In July 1945, the monumental program paid off. At Alamogordo, in the New Mexico desert, scientists finally tested the first atomic device. It was a stunning success: the crash broke windows 125 miles away, and a blind woman saw the light from the explosion. The next month the first two atomic weapons were dropped on Hiroshima and Nagasaki in Japan in an effort to end the war.

MOBILIZATION AND THE BUSINESS COMMUNITY

Mobilization on all fronts worked because business interests were squarely behind the effort. Businessmen had fallen on hard times during the Great Depression, and had found their reputations tarnished. Roosevelt himself had lashed out at them during the 1930s, when he perceived they were resisting governmental programs aimed at promoting recovery. Businessmen, he once said, "are unanimous in their hatred for me—and I welcome their hatred." Though FDR never intended to dismantle the capitalist system, he could, in the country's worst economic crisis, afford angry, anticapitalist rhetoric when it suited his ends. Now, however, he needed business's help.

Secretary of War Henry L. Stimson, a Republican in a Democratic administration, understood exactly what was necessary to meet production requirements. "If you are going to try to go to war, or to prepare for war, in a capitalist country," he said, "you have got to let business make money out of the process or business won't work." The government therefore chose to work on businessmen's terms. It provided incentives and tax breaks that effectively underwrote the expense of plant expansion. Business was permitted to depreciate the cost of conversion over a five-year period in a way that cut back on its taxable income. Firms could recover excess-profits taxes paid during the war if they could show a postwar loss. One economist later termed the arrangement "the biggest and most resilient cushion in the history of public finance." The government also granted firms immunity from antitrust prosecution if they could show that cooperative arrangements would enhance essential war production.

An even more important incentive for business was the cost-plus-a-fixed-fee system, whereby the government guaranteed all development and production costs as well as paid a percentage profit on the wartime goods produced. With frequent design changes demanded and improvements required, business was understandably reluctant to spend large sums of money that were hard to estimate in advance. As the government suspended competitive bidding, and simply urged chosen firms to do whatever was necessary without regard to cost, business found it could not lose, for the government assumed all the risks. Though this caused a measure of waste, the urgency of military demands allowed the process to continue.

Novelist Harriette Arnow characterized vividly the cost-plus system in her powerful novel, *The Dollmaker* (1954). According to one of the characters:

These big men that owns these factories, th' gover'mint gives em profits on what things cost—six cents on th' dollar I've heard say. So every time they can make a thing cost two dollars stid a one . . . they're six cents ahead, an everybody's happy. Th' more men, th' more plus fer th' owners, th' more money an more men fer them unions, I figger.

Businessmen used their ingenuity to make the most of their unique opportunities. Henry Ford's Willow Run plant gained favorable publicity for its use of midgets within small fuselage and wing spaces. But other entrepreneurs, as John Morton Blum has revealed (*V Was for Victory: Politics and American Culture During World War II*, 1976), were even more successful in using war demands for economic gain.

Robert Woodruff, head of Coca-Cola, persuaded the army and navy that Coke was an essential drink well suited to the needs of soldiers and sailors. Though sugar was in short supply on the home front, he was able to get what he needed and to carry syrup, bottles, and in time the entire production process overseas wherever troops went. Woodruff developed such a universal taste for

Coca-Cola, it became and remained the most extensively distributed mass-produced product in the United States.

Philip K. Wrigley, the chewing gum magnate, was equally successful in identifying his product as an essential war good. He supplied a stick of gum for each K ration package, and even agreed to pack the containers in his own plants. At the same time, he sought to market gum to civilians by playing on the military dimension. His advertisements stressed that gum could help war workers, just like soldiers, relax in periods of stress. "To help your workers feel better—work better," he said, "just see that they get five sticks of chewing gum every day."

Then there was Henry J. Kaiser, the shipbuilder who became something of a hero for his ability to get things done. Previously part of a consortium—the Six Companies—that had built the Boulder, Bonneville, and Grand Coulee Dams, he now turned his attention to ships. Using his contacts and connections as well as huge amounts of government capital, he produced tankers, troop ships, landing ships, and destroyer escorts—in sum, 30 percent of the ships built in 1943. He became known for his Liberty ships—merchant vessels made by mass-production methods—which became the major wartime cargo carriers. Prefabrication was the key. In 1941 construction time was 355 days. Kaiser cut that down to 56 days the next year and even turned out a vessel in 14 days in a remarkable demonstration of speed. Though one ship failed dramatically on the pier before sailing, Kaiser's reputation remained untainted.

All sorts of businessmen with expertise to contribute streamed into Washington, D.C., to work in the agencies and commissions responsible for coordinating the production process at the national level. "Dollar-a-year" men were permitted to stay on their company payrolls to preclude their sacrificing regular incomes while they worked for the federal government. They came by the thousands. Eventually, these men made up three-fourths of the executive staff of the War Production Board.

In the cabinet, Henry Stimson and Secretary of the Navy Frank Knox staffed their departments with men from New York and Boston corporate law firms and investment banking houses.

John Lord O'Brien, Robert Lovett, John J. McCloy, Robert Patterson, and James Forrestal were among those who assumed positions of prominence. All of these men kept national interests in mind as they worked on behalf of the war effort; but they also brought with them different assumptions about the nature and role of government than those held by New Dealers in the 1930s. They believed in big business, in its ability to get things done, and in its need to be relatively unhampered by centralized restrictions. Their values had been challenged before, when the public interest had been more vocally expressed, but with national production requirements to be met those values now gained ascendency. Business leaders found they had a relatively free hand to use their own channels and connections in the interest of winning the war. Inevitably, governmental priorities changed.

Under the influence of business interests, there was a good deal of centralization and concentration. Contracts, for example, went to the largest firms, whose operating officers often knew officials in Washington. There were obvious advantages to relying on the nation's major companies. They had the labor pools and assembly lines that could most easily be converted to war production. They also had the research staffs, staffs that could be quickly mobilized to make the necessary refinements in war items. The large firms subcontracted to smaller companies, but inevitably many of the nation's smaller firms, blocked from supplies of scarce materials and unable to produce civilian goods, had to close their doors.

Statistics tell part of the story. *Business Week* declared that after two months of war there were two hundred thousand fewer employers in the nation. It was, the magazine said, the "most severe contraction in the business population that we have ever experienced." According to United States Department of Commerce estimates, three hundred thousand retailers shut down in 1942. Altogether, over half a million small businesses failed during the war.

Meanwhile, the large firms got larger still. In 1940, as the defense program began, 175,000 companies accounted for 70 percent of the nation's manufacturing output, while 100 other companies provided the remaining 30 percent. By March of 1943, with twice as much being produced, the ratio was reversed: now the 100 companies that had produced 30 percent in 1940 held contracts for 70 percent of all defense production.

Congress mandated the creation of a Smaller War Plants Corporation in mid-1942, but it never worked successfully. The corporation's creation was an attempt to legislate a vision of society in which the small entrepreneur had a chance, but that vision gave way in the face of the demand for rapid production to assist in the conduct of the war. Though small businesses hoped for a revival in the postwar period, the creation of an early version of the "military-industrial complex" *during* the struggle provided a framework that favored the industrial giants in the ensuing years.

MOBILIZATION AND WORKERS

Though business interests played a major role in mobilizing the productive might of America during the war, business was not the only sector involved in the process. Without the cooperation of the nation's work force, the United States could never have accomplished the economic miracles that resulted in victory for the Allies.

Workers welcomed the conversion to a war footing, for it heralded an end to the ever-present unemployment of the 1930s. Once the United States began to organize for defense in 1940, jobs became more readily available. Employment opportunities were even greater after the nation entered the war in late 1941.

The work force expanded astronomically to meet production demands. Three times as many men and women joined the military as in World War I, while others quickly took their civilian positions. More than fifteen million people entered either the armed services or the labor force between 1940 and 1943. By the latter year, the unemployment rate stood at 1.3 percent, less than a tenth of the figure in 1937, the *best* year during the Great Depression. Between 1939 and 1945, the number of jobless dropped from nine million to one million, with jobs available to virtually anyone who wanted to work.

One problem that had to be addressed was how to channel workers to jobs where they could be most useful to the war effort. As with the business sector, coordination was necessary in the labor sector. In the spring of 1942, Roosevelt created a War Manpower Commission (WMC), headed by Paul V. McNutt, former governor of Indiana. Its purpose was to try to determine how workers could best be used, but it lacked power to require adherence to directives. At the end of the year, seeking to enhance the commission's authority, the president transferred the selective service to the WMC. Efforts to render work assignments compulsory as a way of making the best use of the labor pool, however, ran into political opposition. Only by the fall of 1943 did the administration come up with a more flexible manpower plan that provided a mechanism for making sure workers were available where needed.

The increased work force buttressed the growing union movement. Labor had come of age during the New Deal in the 1930s. Section 7a of the National Industrial Recovery Act had affirmed labor's right to organize and the National Labor Relations Act—the Wagner Act—had provided the mechanism for union recognition and collective bargaining. The American Federation of Labor (AFL) added millions of workers to its ranks, while the Congress of Industrial Organizations (CIO) undertook to organize basic industry in the United States.

The war enhanced unionization, despite labor's internal splits. In 1935, the CIO broke away from the AFL. As assembly line production made craft distinctions less meaningful, more and more jurisdictional disputes took place. In spite of labor unions' overarching common interests, serious rivalries remained. "We will fight against a movement which has vowed to destroy us and wipe us off the face of the earth," AFL leader William Green declared in late 1941, referring to the CIO. Yet unions of all sorts continued to grow. In the defense period alone union membership increased by 1.5 million, and unions scored a number of impressive gains. In 1941, for example, the United Automobile Workers received a contract from Ford stipulating a "union shop"—a place where workers must be members of a labor organization—and a dues checkoff.

Union growth increased during the war itself. Its membership rose from 10.5 million in 1941 to 14.75 million in 1945. The portion of the work force enrolled in collective bargaining agreements rose from 30 percent to 45 percent. The CIO made the greatest gains. It became established in the major mass-production industries—steel, rubber, automobiles—and was almost the size of the older AFL by the end of the war.

Unions benefited from a "maintenance-of-membership" formula, established by the National War Labor Board (NWLB), which had been created in early 1942 to deal with labor conflicts during the war. Employers, now facing a large labor pool, argued that a union shop deprived workers of the freedom *not* to choose unionization. The NWLB's formula, aimed at securing labor's cooperation, specified that a union member who failed to quit within fifteen days of signing a contract would remain a member for the duration of the contract. That policy preserved a measure of free choice for the worker while protecting union membership levels.

Most historians studying labor trends have acknowledged that industrial union activity came of age during the war. Labor and management, committed to a common goal, learned to talk together, and under government direction, to bargain collectively. The whole process enhanced industrial stability, and provided workers with more job security than they had ever known in the past. At the same time, Nelson Lichtenstein has shown in *Labor's War at Home: The CIO in World War II* (1982), wartime pressures weakened the independence of the industrial union movement and promoted instead routinized forms of bureaucratic activity that made unionism much less militant than it had been in the 1930s.

Still, union members prospered throughout the war. The results were visible in clear economic terms, as workers' wages rose steadily. Average weekly earnings for people involved in manufacturing increased 65 percent—from $32.18 to $47.12 in the 40 months after December 1941. Even after corrections for inflation, real earnings rose 27 percent in manufacturing work. Though there were caps on the increases that were possible in wage rates, total paychecks swelled as employees worked longer hours. The average workweek expanded from 40.6 hours to 45.2 hours between 1941 and 1942; in some factories, the norm became a 50 or 60 hour workweek. Virtually all workers put in some overtime for which they were paid time-and-a-half.

Though they complained about the growing differential between their wage rates and business profits, workers plunged in and did what was necessary to produce the implements of war. Don Johnson, an employee of the AC Spark Plug Division of General Motors in Flint, Michigan, observed later that

After Pearl Harbor there was an immediate change in people's attitude toward their work—their sense of urgency, their dedication, their team work. When the chips were down, people dealt with it like survival. Things that might have taken days longer were done to meet a target so you didn't hold somebody else up—even if it meant putting in extra hours and extra effort.

Johnson went on to describe how right after American entrance into the war, he and others were assigned the task of producing a new item—a navigational computer bomb sight. Though the parent company had doubts about whether the firm could do it, the workers did not: "There was never any doubt on our part that we would do what we'd committed ourselves to do. We just did not accept 'Can't do.'"

Farmers too played an important part in the mobilization process. The overall farm population declined by 17 percent during the war. Millions of Americans left their land to join the armed forces or work in urban factories. Clovis Nevels, one of the major characters in the novel, *The Dollmaker,* reflected this migration away from the farm as he left Kentucky to work in the factories of Detroit.

Those who stayed behind prospered. According to Walter W. Wilcox (*The Farmer in the Second World War,* 1947), they managed to put the specter of depression behind them. After following the policy of crop restriction (in a government effort to promote price stability) during the 1930s, they now found themselves encouraged to produce more and more. They extended the use of commercial fertilizer and embarked on other soil and crop improvements that increased yields during the war years. As they added to their stores of mechanical equipment—tractors, trucks, grain combines—they were able to expand crop acreage. Using scientific knowledge and technological advances, farmers met the wartime demands for more food.

They also secured government support for high farm prices. Through the Farm Bureau Federation, a lobbying organization, and the farm bloc in Congress, they successfully pressed for standards that benefited them. Farmers had prospered between 1910 and 1914, and the ratio between agricultural and industrial prices in those years had come to be defined as "parity." In early 1942, Congress acceded to farmers' pressure in return for votes needed to establish other controls, and set farm price ceilings at 110 percent of parity. During the war, farm prices more than doubled.

With that congressional assistance, and costs checked by other controls, farmers' profits soared. Net farm income increased from $5.3 billion in 1939 to $13.6 billion in 1944. During the war years, per-capita farm income tripled, while per-capita industrial income only doubled.

Farmers finally had a chance to improve their material circumstances. They could reduce indebtedness, leave positions of tenancy, and build new structures only imagined before. Laura Briggs, a member of a farm family from Idaho, noted that "as farm prices got better and better, the farmers suddenly became the wealth of the community. . . . Farm times became good times. Dad started having his land improved, and of course we improved our home and the outbuildings. We and most other farmers went from a tar-paper shack to a new frame house with indoor plumbing."

World War II brought the farmers a new prosperity as they contributed their resources to the process of mobilization and production, and benefited from the results. Like members of other groups, they managed to extricate themselves from the troubling cycles of the Great Depression and to enjoy better times after years of poverty and despair. For the farmers, the war period was a time agricultural historians have come to call the "second American agricultural revolution."

MOBILIZATION: MONEY AND ITS RESULTS

In all areas, mobilization succeeded because government was willing to spend whatever was necessary to win the war. Expenditures rose as never before. Total federal outlays increased from $8.9 billion in 1939 to $95.2 billion in 1945, and simultaneously the gross national product rose from $90.5 billion to $211.9 billion.

"Where's the money coming from?" economist Stuart Chase asked in 1942. "Nobody gives a damn. That is just the point. In the old economy, such reckless outlays would have spelled bankruptcy and ruin. Money came first and men came second. In the new economy, no nation will permit bankruptcy and ruin so long as men, materials, and energy are available. Men first, money second."

In fact, the money came from a number of sources. The war was financed by both taxation and borrowing. Taxes, which had defrayed 30 percent of the cost of World War I, accounted for almost 50 percent of the cost of World War II. Roosevelt would have preferred to have used taxes to cover the entire cost. "I would rather pay one hundred percent of taxes now than push the burden of this war onto the shoulders of my grandchildren," he declared at the end of 1942. But the tax structure was inadequate, and the United States was obliged to borrow the rest of what it needed. That money came from both banks and private investors. The sale of war bonds was one important source of income. The U.S. Treasury Department raised $12.9 billion in the first war loan drive in late 1942, and $135 billion with the entire series of drives.

Wartime spending made a difference in the economic realm.

Economic historians such as Robert Lekachman (*The Age of Keynes*, 1966), among others, have shown how such spending brought the return of prosperity to the United States. The enormous mobilization effort proved to be the stimulus the country had been lacking for so long. Deliberate, sustained, countercyclical spending brought just the improvement that English economist John Maynard Keynes had predicted.

Keynes published his major work, *The General Theory of Employment, Interest and Money*, in 1936, but even earlier he had lectured about the same ideas found in this book to his Cambridge University students. He argued that depression was more than but one phase in the business cycle that would improve in time. Rather, Keynes claimed, depression was equilibrium at a very low level and would persist unless enough spending occurred to get the system moving again. Funds could come from the private sector, through traditional forms of investment, or from the public sector, in the form of aggressive government spending programs or sizable tax cuts. Anything that increased the amount of money in circulation could work.

Keynes met with Roosevelt in 1934, but the two men misunderstood one another. "He left a whole rigmarole of figures," the president commented of Keynes. "He must be a mathematician rather than a political scientist." Keynes in turn had "supposed the President was more literate, economically speaking." For all of the activity during the New Deal, Keynesian theory was never really tried; the nation never committed itself to the deficit spending that could have ended the depression. Conflicting priorities comprised a commitment to recovery alone. The various government initiatives of the 1930s worked in conflicting and contradictory ways, bringing relief to those hardest hit and reform to the system, but failing to generate the needed economic revival.

Then, in 1940, the massive spending that Keynes had called for began to take place. When the United States started to mobilize for defense, the economy improved overnight. "Retail sales began to jump, factories began howling for men, unemployment figures tumbled downhill," Stuart Chase noted. "The backbone of the depression was broken." That improvement gave cause for optimism about the future. "We have seen the last of our great depressions," wartime administrator Chester Bowles declared, "for the simple reason that the public [is] wise enough to know it doesn't have to stand for one."

The results as the economy moved into full gear were stupendous. The huge goals for 1942—60,000 planes, 45,000 tanks, 20,000 antiaircraft guns, and 8,000,000 tons of merchant shipping—were raised still higher for the next year; now the president called for 125,000 planes, 75,000 tanks, 35,000 antiaircraft guns, and 10,000,000 tons of merchant shipping. And the industrial system responded by producing what was needed.

Productivity rose. In 1944, there were 12.5 percent more people in the work force producing 57 percent more goods. In the manufacturing sector, productivity increased 25 percent between 1939 and 1944, compared to an average yearly rise of 1.9 percent in the period between 1889 and 1939. According to the Department of Commerce, output per worker was one-third greater in 1943 than it had been in 1939.

The index of industrial production reflected the gains. From 1935 to 1939 the index equaled 100 and rose to 239 during the war years. In the durable manufactured goods sector, it reached 360.

In every area the figures told the same story. By the middle of 1945, the United States had produced eighty thousand landing craft, one hundred thousand tanks and armored cars, three hundred thousand airplanes, 15 million guns, and 41 billion rounds of ammunition. Production consumed 434 million tons of steel. It also resulted in two atomic bombs.

Never before had American industry operated at full tilt. But now there was no concern about overproduction. Output alone, to the degree possible, was all that mattered as the United States attempted to make whatever materials were necessary to defeat the Axis powers.

Industrial success was complemented in the agricultural sector as well. Livestock output increased 23 percent, crop output 14 percent. Between 1940 and 1945, there was a 36 percent increase in productivity as the number of persons supplied per farm worker rose from 10.7 to 14.6. Farmers who had worried about raising too much in the past now found themselves called on to produce all they could, a call to which they responded enthusiastically.

America's extraordinary productive capacity, and its ability to harness and develop that capacity relatively quickly, made the difference in the war. A year after Pearl Harbor, the nation was producing more than all its enemies combined. At the Teheran Conference in 1943, Soviet leader Joseph Stalin's toast singled out the accomplishments of the United States: "To American production, without which this war would have been lost."

Mobilization had not been easy, but with time it had been accomplished. Reluctance and hesitation had been overcome as the difficult process of conversion took place. As enormous changes occurred, the industrial system became more regimented than it had ever been before. The federal government came to provide the kind of centralized direction it had sought to give in World War I, but this time that direction was carried even farther. Agency followed agency, as FDR tried first one expedient, then another, until he found a system of coordination that worked. The bureaucratic lines were often blurred, as was so often the case during Roosevelt's tenure. The important point, however, is that the system worked in the end. Scarce materials found their way to the plants where they were needed most, and were crafted into the products required for the fight.

With the proper incentives, business did what was necessary on all fronts; and business leaders reveled in their regained positions of prominence and prestige. Even as they occasionally grumbled about controls, they took advantage of the system to make the profits they had missed in the preceding decade: they could only be satisfied with the results of their efforts. Workers were delighted to be employed once more, often in positions more responsible or challenging than before. They too grumbled about limitations and constraints, and sought higher wages than either business or government was willing to grant. But, as they enjoyed the ancillary benefits of the struggle, they had to acknowledge that they were better off than they had been in the past.

And so the United States mobilized for war. Mobilization provided the framework within which all home-front activity unfolded. It brought the revival of prosperity, and raised spirits that had flagged during the depression years. It generated new opportunities for assorted segments of the work force and thereby created expectations for the postwar years. It also conditioned the political climate as new officials gained prominence in the productive effort and new issues had to be confronted in the electoral realm. Mobilization was a major part of the home-front experience. It changed American society as much as it decided the outcome of the war.

TWO

American Society at War

The United States was more fortunate than most other nations involved in World War II. American soldiers fought overseas, and virtually every family had someone in uniform—but no battles took place on American shores. For the most part, the home-front population was far more comfortable than it had been in the preceding decade. Mobilization brought the return of prosperity, and with it the hope and confidence in the American way that had all but disappeared during the Great Depression. Within the United States, the wartime mood was buoyant.

Americans participated in the war in countless ways. The government encouraged their involvement in campaigns and drives intended both to collect necessary resources and to give people a sense of identification with a common cause. Wartime employees worked hard and accomplished the required miracles of production, but they still had money to spend on themselves and time to enjoy what they could again buy.

Of course, some faced problems. Migration to cities where there was war work brought dislocation and discomfort to many. Employees, while appreciating their paychecks, still complained—and struck—when wages fell behind profits as industrialists got rich. Workers in new war plants often found housing conditions uncomfortable at best since building seldom kept pace with population growth. Still, on balance, Americans prospered during the war, and prosperity was reflected by the wartime mood.

WARTIME MOOD AND MORALE

Americans had a sense of shared purpose once they entered the war. Oral histories have added an important dimension to the study of the struggle by showing how ordinary Americans reacted and responded. First-person accounts, particularly those by Studs Terkel (*"The Good War": An Oral History of World War II,* 1984), and by Mark Jonathon Harris, Franklin D. Mitchell, and Steven J. Schechter (*The Homefront: America during World War II,* 1984), have underscored the feeling of commitment. The Japanese attack on Pearl Harbor on December 7, 1941, brought a sense of unity to the United States. The nation had been divided in the late 1930s as the rest of the world moved toward war. Isolationists in America shunned involvement in the larger struggle and resisted the administration's progressive actions to provide the materials antifascist nations needed for their defense, claiming that the United States was committing itself inevitably to war.

The Pearl Harbor attack—which came without warning, knocked out five battleships, ten smaller warships, and left 2,400 servicemen dead—jolted the nation. Initially, Americans felt sheer shock; then shock turned to rage. Millions never forgot where they were or what they were doing when they heard the news. Don Johnson, a Flint, Michigan, citizen, echoed the sentiments many held as he recalled his reactions after learning of the catastrophe: "First it was indignation, then it turned to anger, and by the time one went to work the following morning it was determination: 'They can't do that to us.'"

Some were afraid. Rumors were rife: The number of damaged ships increased as the story was retold, and other imaginary destruction was described. Dennis Keegan, a student at the University of San Francisco, came home to find his landlady screaming, "Dennis, turn the lights out! The Japs are comin'! The Japs are comin'! The Golden Gate Bridge has been bombed."

Americans recognized almost instinctively that Pearl Harbor marked a turning point in their lives. After the attack, nothing would ever be the same. War meant adjustments to new patterns, disruptions to be overcome. And it forced a rapid growing up. Jean Bartlett, a fourteen year old from Berkeley, California, later recalled: "On December 6, 1941, I was playing with paper dolls: Deanna Durbin, Sonja Henie. I had a Shirley Temple doll that I cherished. After Pearl Harbor, I never played with dolls again."

Franklin Roosevelt gave focus to Americans' feelings as he addressed Congress the next day. Calling December 7 "a date which will live in infamy," he asked Congress to declare "that since the unprovoked and dastardly attack . . . a state of war has existed." Sixty million Americans listening to their radios heard the president's speech. They understood that long-smoldering tensions had led to an unavoidable war.

At the same time, they felt a sense of relief; the period of waiting was finally over. Now the nation could commit itself more fully to the task at hand. Secretary of War Stimson summed up the prevailing sentiments of most of those in the government when he said, "My first feeling was of relief that the indecision was over and that a crisis had come in a way which would unite all our people." The attack created a sense of common danger that drew people together for the lengthy struggle ahead. A *Newsweek*

headline read: "AMERICANS ALL: National Disunity is Ended."
A University of Oregon student declared: "We're all together
now; that ought to be worth a couple of battleships."

Americans, John Morton Blum (*V Was for Victory*) has suggested, were largely in agreement on their aims in the war. Victory was, without question, the preeminent concern of policy-
makers and the public alike, yet there was a series of more
specific aims to which most people subscribed. Even before the
United States entered the war, in a message to Congress in early
1941, FDR had spoken of the "four essential human freedoms"—
freedom of speech and expression, freedom of worship, freedom
from want, and freedom from fear. In the summer of that year, in
the Atlantic Charter, Roosevelt and British Prime Minister Win-
ston Churchill had laid out their vision of the postwar world, a
vision in which the self-determination of nations, equal trading
rights for all, and a system of general security would prevail.

Those declarations helped define the war's *formal* mission.
But most Americans—at home as well as on the battlefield—
fought the war for more personal ends. Though they wanted to
defeat the dictators—from Hitler to Hirohito—they saw the
struggle not simply in ideological terms but with respect to what
they knew best. They wanted to protect their own patterns of existence, mundane though they may have been. They clung to a
vision of home above all else as they struggled to make their way
of life secure. John Hersey, a war correspondent, while reporting
on marines on Guadalcanal, asked one young soldier why he was
fighting. The GI paused, then responded, "Jesus, what I'd give
for a piece of blueberry pie." For Hersey, that comment reflected
both nostalgia and a commitment to home: Soldiers, like others,
were committed to the patterns they knew. They were fighting to
preserve what they most valued; they wanted a better past.

Americans saw the war in black and white terms. In 1942,
anthropologist Margaret Mead observed that for people in the
United States to make the necessary commitment, "we must feel
that we are on the side of the Right." During the war, Americans
felt that virtue was on their side. James Covert, a nine year old
from Portland, Oregon, when the war began, later recalled his

view of the struggle: "To me it was like a medieval morality play. They were bad, we were good, and God was on our side." Poet Archibald MacLeish was somewhat more eloquent. For him, the war was "in its essence a revolt of man against himself—a revolt of stunted, half-formed, darkened men against a human world beyond their reach and most of all against the human world of reason and intelligence and sense."

The United States conveyed its war goals through an organized propaganda program, described first by Allan M. Winkler in *The Politics of Propaganda: The Office of War Information, 1942–1945* (1978), that focused on securing support both at home and abroad. Propaganda provided a means through which the nation defined its priorities and communicated them as broadly as possible. Yet the program suffered from the same administrative difficulties that characterized other efforts in the Roosevelt government: agencies constantly competing with one another, conflicting lines of authority, and general chaos until the middle of 1942.

From the time war broke out in Europe, Roosevelt tried first one propaganda measure, then another, just as he had on the mobilization front. An Office of Government Reports, established in September 1939, acted as a clearinghouse for requests for material from the government about its activities. The Division of Information of the Office of Emergency Management, set up in March 1941, served as the chief source of information about the government's defense activities. When neither of those agencies functioned particularly well, the president created an Office of Facts and Figures—superimposed on both the above agencies—in October 1941, under the direction of Archibald MacLeish. Its purpose: to coordinate the presentation of materials pertaining to national defense. On the overseas front, playwright Robert Sherwood established a Foreign Information Service in the Office of the Coordinator of Information in August of the same year.

Despite those efforts (or perhaps because of them), the propaganda program was in a state of shambles in the first months of America's formal involvement in the war. To deal with that situation, in June 1942 Roosevelt finally created a new Office of War

Information (OWI), which assumed the functions of all the other, earlier organizations. Heading the agency was news commentator Elmer Davis, a man known to millions of Americans for his clear delivery and dry humor in his nightly radio broadcasts on CBS.

Although OWI ran into resistance from the start—particularly from Republicans who viewed it as a publicity arm to promote a fourth term for FDR—it did manage to convey the nation's aims in the war. It trumpeted the liberal terms of the Four Freedoms and the Atlantic Charter. Even more important, it reflected the war Americans were fighting by summing up American values and communicating them to audiences at home and abroad. OWI portrayed Americans as they wanted to be seen. The prevailing view was that they were sympathetic, even sentimental. They combined "an idealistic aspiration toward Utopia with shrewd, hard, horse sense. . . . They are slow to anger, but, once aroused, they finish what they start." Americans were, according to OWI, "an aggressive people, tough and virile—who can take the initiative, who hit hard and like to hit hard." Having conquered a continent, they were now ready to conquer their enemies in the war.

OWI pictured American society in flattering ways. Through radio messages, leaflets, booklets, and films, it described the industrial miracles taking place as the United States created the greatest fighting machine ever known. *Victory,* a glossy OWI magazine, told of one factory producing a 4-engine bomber every hour as it let the world know that two million men would soon fight in 185,000 American planes. OWI's film *Autobiography of a Jeep* told in sixteen different languages the story of the vehicle that came to symbolize American involvement in the war wherever it went.

Propaganda constantly sought to generate an appreciation for the American way of life. OWI issued stories on everything from ballet to baseball. It showed Americans engaged in such diverse activities as fighting boll weevils, governing themselves, and going to church. The treatment was overwhelmingly positive. There were obvious faults in American society. But even while reporting problems to the rest of the world, OWI slanted them so that the larger picture remained hopeful as it portrayed the America that ordinary citizens wanted to maintain.

And in everything it issued, OWI communicated the sense of confidence that Americans felt. In his message asking for a declaration of war after Pearl Harbor, Franklin Roosevelt proclaimed his abiding faith that "we will gain the inevitable triumph—so help us God." OWI echoed that faith. Its basic message, according to Elmer Davis, was "that we are coming, that we are going to win, and that in the long run everybody will be better off because we won."

OWI was not the only organization trying to generate support for the war effort. An Office of Civilian Defense (OCD) was similarly involved in trying to boost American morale, even as it sought to protect civilians from attack by involving them in civil defense programs. Set up in May 1941 under the direction of New York Mayor Fiorello La Guardia, OCD worked in a variety of ways to encourage participation in the war.

La Guardia was most interested in the air raid protection aspect of his organization. Even before Pearl Harbor, he moved to set up local defense councils in cities and towns, but that early program was barely adequate. After the Japanese strike, however, Americans grew fearful of further attacks: they saw German submarines cruising off the East Coast, and they were aware of Japanese submarine activity off the West Coast. In a February 1942 press conference, the president fueled those fears when he responded to a question about the possibility of an enemy attack. The enemy, he replied, "can come in and shell New York tomorrow night, under certain conditions. They can probably . . . drop bombs on Detroit tomorrow night, under certain conditions." In the months that followed, the civil defense effort became more systematic and began to bring results. Cities participated in blackouts to protect themselves from possible attack, and ground observers scanned the skies for enemy planes.

Air raid protection, however, was only a part of OCD's mandate. Roosevelt also intended the agency to boost morale. A Voluntary Participation Program, directed by Eleanor Roosevelt, the president's wife, soon ran into trouble. Mrs. Roosevelt appointed

Mayris Chaney, a dancer, and Melvyn Douglas, a liberal and outspoken actor, to her staff. Political opponents attacked Chaney as a "fan dancer" and "stripteaser" and Douglas as a fellow traveler and communist sympathizer. In the face of those attacks, Mrs. Roosevelt and her associates resigned.

Yet OCD continued to encourage citizen involvement in the struggle. In the spring of 1942, it sponsored a series of "town meetings for war," staged presentations that were aimed at promoting participation. It also supported the numerous campaigns that sought to motivate home-front Americans to do their part in the war.

CAMPAIGNS AND POPULAR CULTURE

There were various campaigns, first described in detail by Richard R. Lingeman in *Don't You Know There's a War On? The American Home Front, 1941–1945* (1970). The government wanted to channel civilian energies into useful tasks, so it encouraged people to save scarce resources whenever they could. Homemakers, for example, were cajoled to save kitchen fats and turn them in to the butcher. One pound of fat presumably contained enough glycerin to manufacture a pound of black powder that could be used for shells or bullets.

Americans participated in scrap metal drives. Many followed instructions and collected tin cans or conserved in other ways. If each American family bought one less can a week, the argument went, that would save 2,500 tons of tin and 1,900 tons of steel, which in turn could be used to produce 5,000 tanks or 38 Liberty ships. The iron in one old shovel could be converted into four hand grenades. Razor blades contained steel that could be recycled and made into machine guns; old lipstick tubes contained brass that could be reused in cartridges. Eager to play their part, citizens resorted to ingenious schemes to provide the necessary metal. In Virginia, they raised sunken ships from the James River. In Wyoming, they dismantled an old steam engine and built a road so they could collect the parts.

When rubber was in short supply, they gathered used materials and turned them in. In June 1942, the president asked people at home to collect "old tires, old rubber raincoats, old garden hose, rubber shoes, bathing caps, gloves—whatever you have that is made of rubber." Some got caught up in the spirit of the drive. The manager of a radio station in New York voiced his delight when "a carload of girls from a musical comedy drove up here and they busted off garter straps, wriggled out of girdles and what not. This is fun!"

Still another campaign encouraged Americans to buy bonds to help finance the war. In the spring of 1941, Roosevelt permitted a campaign initiated by Secretary of the Treasury Henry Morgenthau, Jr. "to use *bonds* to sell the *war*." On September 21, 1943, singer Kate Smith played her part in a radio drive. Speaking sixty-five times between 8:00 A.M. and 2:00 A.M. the next morning to an audience of some twenty million people, she raised about $39 million.

Other bond drives followed. The seven war loans were all oversubscribed, though government officials were disappointed that individual quotas went unfilled while institutions—banks and corporations—took up the slack. In their effort to encourage individual involvement and investment, organizers often resorted to stunts. Auctioneers, for example, traded celebrity items—actor Jack Benny's violin, actress Betty Grable's stockings, racehorse Man o' War's shoes—in return for pledges to buy bonds.

On still another front, Americans were encouraged to plant Victory gardens in which they could grow their own food. That program was enormously popular. At its height, there were nearly twenty million such gardens. Some consisted of large fields; others were tiny plots. In 1943, these gardens provided more than a third of all the vegetables grown in the country. New foods such as Swiss chard and kohlrabi found their way onto American tables.

Not all gardens were successful, but it was the spirit that counted. Sheril Jankovsky Cunning, who grew up in Long Beach, California, during the war, recalled her family's garden: "We had the most miserable, hard-as-cement, three-by-five-foot plot of ground, and grew radishes and carrots as our contribution to the war. But radishes weren't anybody's mainstay, and our carrots never got bigger than an inch. Yet we all wanted to do our part for the war. You got caught up in the mesmerizing spirit of patriotism."

Conserve and collect. Play your part. Do what is necessary to support the war. In drive after drive, Americans were encouraged to "Use it up, wear it out, make it do or do without." To those who resisted or proved reluctant, the refrain "Don't you know there's a war on?" followed.

Most home-front Americans, as Richard Polenberg (*War and Society: The United States, 1941–1945*, 1972) and Geoffrey Perrett (*Days of Sadness, Years of Triumph: The American People, 1939–1945*, 1973) have shown, were comfortable during the war. They shared a feeling of well-being that had been missing a decade earlier. Demographic patterns reflected their improved mood. Working at well-paying jobs once again, young people who had chosen to postpone marriage or family during the depression now ceased to wait. Population, which had grown by only 3 million in the 1930s, increased by 6.5 million between 1940 and 1945. The postwar baby boom began during the war.

Popular music trumpeted American optimism. "Goodbye, Momma, I'm off to Yokohama," proclaimed one song. "Praise the Lord and Pass the Ammunition," echoed another. "There's a Star Spangled Banner Waving Somewhere" was one of the largest-selling records in the country in 1942 and 1943. Americans seeking a song like "Over There," which had so captured their eagerness and summed up their confidence in World War I, never found one. Instead, the music industry ground out a series of trite and forgettable titles: "You're a Sap, Mister Jap"; "Let's Take a Rap at the Jap"; "The Japs Don't Have a Chinaman's Chance"; and "We're Gonna Find a Feller Who Is Yeller and Beat Him Red, White, and Blue." The sentimental favorite had nothing to do with fighting or with the war itself. "White Christmas," first heard in 1942 in the film *Holiday Inn*, was soon sung by soldiers in hot desert jungles as well as by civilians in the United States. Like blueberry pie, the song represented home.

Americans, working at full-tilt during the war, sought new ways to spend the money they once again had. They could now afford items they had done without in the depression years, only to find out that much of what they wanted was in short supply as the country converted to the production of war goods. Some saved their money, as evidenced by bank deposits reaching a new high; others paid off mortgages and debts; and still others found new ways to dispose of new income.

"People want to spend money," a store manager noted, "and if they can't spend it on textiles they'll spend it on furniture; or . . . we'll find something else for them." In 1942, they spent $95 million on pharmaceuticals, $20 million more than the year before. They were no sicker; they simply had money to spare. The average department store sale rose from $2.00 before the war to $10.00 during the struggle. On December 7, 1944—the third anniversary of Pearl Harbor—R. H. Macy & Company in New York enjoyed the biggest selling day it had ever had.

People bought books in greater numbers. Paper was in short supply, so publishers used smaller type and issued fewer titles. Even so, sales rose as a mass market developed. Every year after Pearl Harbor, the number of books sold rose by more than 20 percent. Publishers in 1943 did 40 percent better than the year before; membership in the Book-of-the-Month Club doubled during the war.

A new market for paperback books—introduced in 1939 by the Pocket Book Company—developed. Sales increased astronomically, jumping from several hundred thousand to ten million books in 1941, then rising to twenty million in 1942 and forty million in 1943. Avon and Dell also capitalized on the growing demand. Murder mysteries were the most popular—150,000 sold per week—with self-help and health books coming next.

The publishing phenomenon of the war was *One World* by Wendell Willkie, defeated Republican presidential candidate in 1940. His book, issued in the fall of 1943 after he returned from a tour of the Soviet Union, China, the Middle East, and North and South America, was a plea for harmony and a call for hope in the postwar world. It sold faster than any book in publishing history. Simon and Schuster had anticipated selling 200,000 copies; that printing was gone in seventy-two hours. A million copies—both hardbound and softbound—sold in two months; two million copies sold in two years. *"One World* was probably the most influential book published in America during the war," wrote one reviewer. "Like *Uncle Tom's Cabin* it was part of the country."

Americans also enjoyed comic books. Sales rose from twelve million copies a month in 1942 to over sixty million a month in 1946. Eighty percent of the population aged six to seventeen read comic books during the war; a third of people from eighteen to thirty years of age did the same. Seventy million people followed their heroes in daily newspaper comic strips. Publishers catered to both a children's and a servicemen's market; a special edition of *Superman* went overseas.

Comics, like books and other forms of entertainment, reflected common concerns. Americans continued to be amused by the antics of comic book characters, as they had been in the past, and enjoyed watching them confront many of the same problems real people faced every day.

Most comic heroes participated in the war: Joe Palooka, Dick Tracy, and others enlisted in the military services and did their part. But not all characters became involved on the fighting front. Superman sat out the war, for his creators worried that he would make the struggle seem too easy, given the hardships faced by real soldiers. And so reporter Clark Kent was 4–F for the duration. At his preinduction physical, he failed the eye test when his X-ray vision led him to read the chart in the next room. At home, "Blondie" and "Bringing Up Father" poked fun at the problems of wartime life and encouraged participation in bond and conservation campaigns. Wonder Woman, a new creation in 1941, sought "to save the world from the hatred and wars of men in a man-made world," as she provided a different kind of role model.

Americans went to the movies in record numbers. More than ninety million people attended films each week as admissions increased about 33 percent. Yearly grosses rose well over a billion dollars, even though fears of film shortages caused the total number of films released to drop from 533 in 1942 to 377 in 1945.

Hollywood continued to grind out the entertainment stories that had been popular in peacetime. Some critics, Archibald MacLeish among them, complained that the films were "escapist and delusive," and failed to address the issues of the war. They argued that light musicals like *Star Spangled Rhythm* or *The Yanks Are Coming* showed no sensitivity to larger questions, and that battle pictures like *Stand by for Action* conveyed nothing more than the value of military strength. *Casablanca,* the still popular Humphrey Bogart/Ingrid Bergman film, critics argued, buried ideological concerns beneath Rick's cynicism and gave precedence to romantic concerns. The critics were right, but Hollywood persisted, for its winning formula remained popular during the war.

Americans also spent money on other forms of entertainment. They joined country clubs and golf clubs; they went to racetracks; they frequented nightclubs in increasing numbers. The entertainment business boomed, despite liquor shortages and a federal amusement tax. Big bands were popular. So, too, were performers like Frank Sinatra, a young crooner from Hoboken, New Jersey, who became a sensation. In 1942, at New York's Paramount Theater, huge audiences of bobby-soxers—young teenage girls wearing socks rolled to the ankle—swooned as their hero sang.

Vacations were popular. Americans swarmed to crowded bus depots and train stations as they left for a holiday. East, West, and Gulf Coast beaches were crowded in the summer, and Florida spots were equally attractive in the winter. Those who chose not to go far away found new sites and amusements in areas closer to home.

Americans remained intensely interested in professional sports. Baseball, the national game, was hurt by the war because more than 4,000 of the 5,700 players in the major and minor leagues entered the military services. Still, the game survived. The president recognized its value as a morale builder and encouraged its continuation throughout the war.

The major leagues hung on. Games were played in twilight to allow working fans to attend without violating the ban on night contests that existed in some parts of the country. Teams often featured rosters dramatically different from those in the days before Pearl Harbor. Gone were Joe DiMaggio, Bob Feller, Ted Williams, Hank Greenberg, Peewee Reese, and scores of others. Instead, lineups featured virtual unknowns. One such player was Pete Gray, who joined the St. Louis Browns in 1945. He played in seventy-seven games and hit .218—all with one arm. An able outfielder who caught the ball in his glove, then flipped it up, grabbed it with his bare hand, and threw it back, he could also lay down a good drag bunt. Crowds came to see Gray, who became a major box office attraction.

SHORTAGES AND CONTROLS

The war also brought its problems. Americans, even with money in their pockets, had to endure the disruptions that war created at home. Conditions were far more stable than in England, France, Germany, or the Soviet Union; but they were troublesome nonetheless, particularly in boom times, and Americans were often frustrated by the problems they could not avoid.

Shortages in consumer items irritated everyone. With raw materials diverted to military use, civilians had to make do with less in virtually every area of daily life. Cutbacks even affected clothing styles. Metal for zippers went into guns, rubber for girdles was used for trucks and tanks, and fabric for civilian clothing was necessary for uniforms. Curtailment was therefore necessary in the number and kinds of styles the public could buy.

In March 1942, the War Production Board entered the field of fashion. Anxious to save forty to fifty million pounds of wool a year, the WPB ordered the elimination of vests, patch pockets, cuffs, and an extra pair of trousers in men's suits. It also insisted that suits be single-breasted and feature slightly shorter jackets with narrower lapels. Women's fashions changed as well. Similar government regulations limited width and length of skirts, which meant hemlines began to rise. Styles featured straighter cuts and simpler lines, clothing without ruffles or pleats. Gone were the bathing suits with billowing skirts of the 1930s; two-piece suits were justified on the basis of military need. Fashion retailer Stanley Marcus called the new styles "patriotic chic."

Because silk was a war casualty there were shortages in women's stockings. In 1941, the government embargoed silk that came from Japan. Nylon, used in about 20 percent of all hose, was substituted until that too was diverted, in this case, into the manufacture of parachutes. Although cotton stockings were possible, they never became popular, and in any event, cotton too was scarce. Some women resorted to the not wholly satisfactory expedient of painting stockings on their legs.

Food shortages also bothered Americans. Sugar became scarce as early as December 1941 when imports from the Philippines stopped and shipping shortages hindered the transport of crops from Cuba and Puerto Rico. People began to hoard sugar immediately after Pearl Harbor. Even when Caribbean supplies became available, they failed to keep up with civilian and military demand. A coffee shortage occurred when lack of cargo space prevented its transport from Brazil. Meats and countless other items were similarly in short supply.

Throughout the country, people struggled to make do. They cut back on the amount of sugar they used in food or drink and found substitutes for cooking and baking. Restaurants put less sugar in sugar bowls. To meet the coffee crisis, some establishments began cutting out coffee refills; railroad dining cars served coffee only at breakfast. Meat shortages led some restaurants to try buffalo or antelope steaks—even beaverburgers—as alternatives to more traditional fare.

While the shortages themselves hurt, the larger government concern was that shortages would lead to price increases as supply ran far short of demand. The rapidly increasing federal spending was putting more and more money in circulation, thus causing real fears that inflation would get out of control. And the fears seemed warranted: in the first half of 1942, the cost-of-living index climbed 7 percent. When Roosevelt received the advice that "a little inflation would not hurt," he responded with the story of "a fellow who took a little cocaine and kept coming back for more until he was a drug addict." He remembered the First World War, when prices had risen 62 percent between 1914 and 1918 and another 40 percent in the immediate postwar years. The president was determined not to allow another such spurt.

FDR first attempted to head off inflation-induced trouble when he created the Office of Price Administration and Civilian Supply in April 1941. John Kenneth Galbraith ("Reflections on Price Control," *Quarterly Journal of Economics,* 1949), was one of the first scholars to describe the difficulties that agency faced. Charged with preventing profiteering and price hiking, which could raise the cost of living, the office had only the power of "jawboning"—trying to force compliance by verbal argument alone—and thus proved ineffective. The following January, Congress gave the agency, now called simply the Office of Price Administration (OPA), the power to freeze retail prices and control rents in areas near war plants. When the process of selective controls proved cumbersome, OPA in April 1942 issued the General Maximum Price Regulation, which froze retail prices at the level they had reached in March. Though that ruling too proved hard to enforce, it opened the way to another measure in October of the same year that further broadened price control and provided for wage control as well.

OPA also got into the business of rationing with ten major programs that began in 1942. Rationing came to include such scarce items as sugar, coffee, meat, butter, tires, and gasoline. Ration books, issued by local boards, contained stamps or coupons entitling consumers to purchase different products that were in short supply. Initially, the system worked on a single-item basis; later, it was revised to include a flexible point system that could be adjusted to charge more points for particularly scarce items. The revised system was developed in an effort to bring supply in line with demand.

Consumers grumbled about the rationing program, which seemed to violate the traditional American value of individual choice. Moreover, the rules felt overly restrictive. Some people therefore resorted to the black market, where they had to pay a bit more but could get what they wanted from an agreeable merchant. Black market operations were illegal, of course, but nonetheless involved even respectable proprietors and flourished as Americans struggled with the inconveniences at home.

Despite the complaints, price control worked. Scarce goods were distributed relatively fairly, and inflation was held in check. In the two years after mid-1943, consumer prices rose by less than 2 percent. Though OPA was one of the most unpopular federal agencies, Gallup polls revealed that more than 90 percent of the public approved of some form of price control.

Americans were less sympathetic toward wage control. Workers were unhappy when wages did not seem to keep pace with profits. Though wages rose during the war, thanks in large part to overtime efforts, the gap between wages and profits seemed to grow larger and larger all the time.

Organized labor, Nelson Lichtenstein has observed in *Labor's War at Home,* was particularly unhappy with the regulatory apparatus that placed restrictions on what employees could earn. The president was concerned that wage as much as price increases would fuel inflation. Wages, therefore, had to stay within certain bounds. The National War Labor Board (NWLB), the organization responsible for wage control, adopted the "Little Steel" formula in July 1942. Faced with a wage demand by workers at the Bethlehem, Republic, Youngstown, and Inland steel companies, the NWLB established a formula for wage increases. It took January 1, 1941, as a starting point, then allowed a 15 percent increase to meet the rise in living costs until May 1942. The formula applied elsewhere as well. Since most workers had already received some increase, the formula served to keep inflation in check.

The NWLB retained some discretionary authority to correct inequities, but lost that authority with the president's "hold the line" order in April 1943; wages were no longer to be considered in collective bargaining. When labor protested, some modification was permitted, but the basic outlines of the policy remained and held the rise in wage rates to only 24 percent throughout the war.

Organized labor was troubled, all the more so because labor and business representatives together had agreed on December 23, 1941, to refrain from strikes and lockouts. Made as a patriotic gesture, the no-strike pledge was not binding, but nevertheless had the force of a moral commitment. The pledge became more difficult to sustain as living costs rose. In mid-1943, the Michigan CIO voted to rescind the pledge. The issue had surfaced in 1942, at which time it had been defeated; the next year, however, the outcome was reversed. Though the vote brought no nationwide change, it reflected growing worker dissatisfaction.

Workers, in fact, often simply ignored the pledge. Militancy from below led to wildcat strike activity that increased steadily during the war. The number of strikes and strikers in 1942 was roughly what it had been in the depression years. It more than doubled in 1943 and continued to rise in 1944 and 1945. Altogether, there were 14,471 strikes throughout the country between the time of the attack on Pearl Harbor and the end of the war with Japan. The problem peaked in 1944, when there were more than 2,115,000 workers idle, with about 8,721,000 workdays lost. Most of the strikes were short, lasting only a few days. Nonetheless, they disturbed government officials. "Strikes are spreading at an alarming rate," declared one NWLB member, "and unless they are checked immediately, the 'no-strike—no lockout' agreement will become meaningless."

The most disturbing strikes came in the coal fields. John L. Lewis, head of the United Mine Workers, was a bitter enemy of FDR. Lewis, as Melvin Dubofsky and Warren Van Tine have shown (*John L. Lewis*, 1978), was an outspoken leader. Though he had initially supported both the New Deal and the president, in the late 1930s he became disillusioned with what he felt was the president's overly cautious approach to reform. He opposed Roosevelt's reelection in 1940, and remained determined to advance the interests of his own men. The president had no affection for Lewis either. In late 1941, he termed him a "psychopathic" case, and two years later said that he would be happy to resign if Lewis would commit suicide.

In 1943, Lewis led four hundred thousand bituminous coal miners in strikes on four different occasions. He claimed that the miners had long worked for substandard wages and in substandard conditions. "When the mine workers' children cry for bread," he declared, "they cannot be satisfied with a 'Little Steel' formula." It was a "miserably stupid" arrangement, issued by a board of "labor zombies." He therefore demanded substantial wage concessions.

When management refused to budge, Lewis called three successive walkouts, each lasting several days, in May and June. The government then took over the mines, with Secretary of the Interior Ickes in charge. Each time there was a walkout, work resumed when the administration appealed to the miners' patriotism *and* threatened to end draft deferments if they stayed out on strike.

Lewis was not popular but he was persistent. Though polls in June 1943 showed that 87 percent of the public viewed him unfavorably, he had unanimous rank and file support. In early November, all bituminous coal miners were on strike. Once again, Roosevelt seized the mines, but this time he ordered Ickes to negotiate a contract acceptable to Lewis. Ickes did so, with an agreement that bypassed the restrictions of the "Little Steel" formula. Lewis had won, though the formula remained in force in other areas until the end of the war.

The agitation in the coal fields, however, had consequences that further disturbed members of the labor movement. Conservative elements in Congress, uncomfortable with labor gains of the 1930s, had been looking for an opportunity to limit any further labor advances. With business interests once again in control, the conservatives sensed a shift in political mood. When a dozen states passed measures that restricted labor in 1943, Congress was ready to act.

The War Labor Disputes Act, sponsored by Representative Howard Smith of Virginia and Senator Tom Connally of Texas and known as the Smith-Connally Act, was passed in June 1943.

It required unions to give formal notice of intention to strike, to observe a thirty-day cooling-off period, and then to gain majority membership approval before walking out. The act also gave the president greater power to seize war plants, provided penalties for engaging in illegal work stoppages, and prohibited union gifts to political campaigns. Although Roosevelt vetoed the measure, Congress overrode the veto within a few hours. A measure long desired had become law.

While the Smith-Connally Act never proved as restrictive as its opponents feared, it did reflect a shift in sympathy at the national level. For members of the work force, it proved to be one more irritant during the war.

WARTIME DISLOCATIONS

The war also brought dislocations that disrupted daily life on other fronts. Record numbers of Americans who had left their homes during the struggle were particularly vulnerable. According to Census Bureau estimates, 15.3 million people moved during the war. Net interstate migration between 1940 and 1945 was a million times higher than it had been the half decade before. Some of the travelers were members of servicemen's families trying to stay together as long as they could; others sought jobs in the factories making war implements.

People moved in all directions. Many drifted from south to north; more traveled from east to west. Since half of the nation's shipbuilding and airplane manufacturing activity took place on the Pacific Coast, many of the migrants went in that direction; California attracted 2 million new inhabitants, with the population of the Los Angeles area alone growing by 440,000. Simultaneously, other areas grew. Michigan had a net increase of 287,000 migrants between 1940 and 1943, with much of the concentration found in the Detroit area to which they were attracted by converted automobile plants and airplane factories. Seaport regions in the South expanded as well. In the four years after 1940, the population of the Mobile, Alabama, area grew by 65 percent; the Hampton Roads, Virginia, area by 45 percent; and the Charleston, South Carolina, area by 38 percent. Washington, D.C., flooded with new government workers and dollar-a-year men, grew by 231,000 between 1940 and 1943.

Cities in particular suffered terrible congestion that proved hard to handle. Having been shaken by the Great Depression, they found themselves strained even before they had to gear up for war. Many still had debts to repay and long-overdue civic improvements to make. Now they had to cope with tens or hundreds of thousands of new inhabitants in inadequate houses, hospitals, and schools.

Often, living conditions were grim. Housing developments were crowded and cramped, depressing to those who came from rural regions where they had been accustomed to space. The Nevels family in the novel *The Dollmaker,* migrating from eastern Kentucky to Detroit, settled in a housing project where one building looked like the next, where families could hear one another through thin walls, where the relentless urban environment was impossible to escape. In some trailer areas, particularly around Willow Run, workers who could not find more permanent housing lived with substandard sanitation and constant fear of disease.

Worse than the hostile conditions were the responses of residents disgruntled by the crowding in of migrants that disrupted their lives. Rural migrants found themselves branded "hillbillies." Cruel tales circulated about Southerners who arrived in Detroit without shoes or who dropped letters in fire alarm boxes. "Before the bomber plant was built, everything was perfect here," one Willow Run resident observed. "Everybody knew everybody else and all were happy and contented. Then came that bomber plant and all this influx of riffraff, mostly Southerners. You can't be sure of these people." The newcomers themselves were equally unhappy. "We found Detroit a cold city, a city without a heart or a soul," David Crockett Lee wrote to his local newspaper. "So we are going back to Tennessee . . . where men and women are neighborly, and where even the stranger is welcome."

Housing was perhaps the most serious problem. Adequate housing was in short supply. Even before the war began, many cities were in trouble. A 1938 WPA survey revealed that 70,000 of Detroit's 414,000 dwelling units were substandard. With the huge population increase during the war, the situation became intolerable. Conditions were the same all over. In Hartford, Connecticut, ten thousand additional units were needed in 1942.

Families were often reduced to living together in a single room. A San Francisco city official observed in 1943: "Families are sleeping in garages, with mattresses right on cement floors and three, four, five to one bed." Shantytowns, like the Hoovervilles of the Great Depression, sprang up, with inadequate sewage facilities and a lack of basic necessities.

The federal effort to build more housing became bogged down in bureaucratic disputes. These were largely undescribed until the publication of Philip J. Funigiello's *The Challenge to Urban Liberalism: Federal-City Relations during World War II* (1978). New Deal reformers wanted to use public housing to revitalize cities, abolish slums, and eliminate urban poverty. During the war, their priorities clashed with those of presidential appointees who wanted to build structures to accommodate new workers as quickly and expeditiously as possible. Congress came down on the side of speed, as fiscal conservatives had little sympathy with what they termed "socialistic experiments," and sought to ensure that public housing would not compete with private enterprise in the postwar period.

For eighteen months little progress was made in coping with the problem. Then, in February 1942, Roosevelt finally consolidated sixteen different housing organizations into one National Housing Agency (NHA). It soon decided on the construction of temporary structures, and that policy held for the duration of the war. Once underway, a great deal of building occurred. The government spent $2.3 billion in a massive construction effort, as the NHA erected 832,000 units to accompany the 1 million units built by private companies. The agency also located existing vacant housing when it could. While the effort did not wholly meet wartime needs, it did succeed in dealing with the most serious conditions.

Familial and moral stress also plagued Americans during the

war. Families suffered the strains of separation as soldiers went overseas. The Bureau of Labor Statistics estimated the breakup of more than three million families by April 1944. The divorce rate rose from 16 per 100 marriages in 1940 to 27 per 100 in 1944. Never before—not even during the Great Depression—had American families been subjected to such stress.

Inadequate day-care facilities complicated the lives of working mothers. Shortages were severe. For a long time the subject was unstudied, but in recent years more attention has been paid to social conditions during the war. Karen Anderson in particular, in *Wartime Women: Sex Roles, Family Relations, and the Status of Women during World War II* (1981), has documented the difficulties faced. In Seattle, in late 1942, there were but seven WPA nurseries and three private establishments serving 350 children, with 75,000 women in the work force. In Tacoma, only one day-care center accommodated twenty thousand women. The Lanham Act of 1940 provided federal funds for expanding war communities, but bureaucratic procedures were cumbersome and slow. Still, by the war's end, the government had spent $52 million on 3,102 centers for 600,000 children in the largest commitment to child care the nation had ever made. Though that hardly met the total need, it was a start. Yet even the provision of day-care facilities did not ensure their use. Some mothers were reluctant to put their children in institutional settings, so they worked out a variety of other makeshift arrangements.

With children on their own more, juvenile delinquency became a serious problem and truancy rates rose. In Detroit, the truancy rate jumped 24 percent between 1938 and 1943. High school enrollment across the country dropped by more than a million from 1941 to 1944. Juvenile crime rates rose, with theft, property damage, and sexual misconduct the major offenses.

More staid Americans were worried about the actions of "victory girls"—young women who flaunted traditional moral codes and attached themselves to servicemen when they could. While promiscuity was not as serious as prostitution, it was still a source of concern among those committed to conventional mores. In 1942, more than twice as many girls under twenty-one were arrested for sexual offenses—not prostitution—than in the year before.

Venereal disease was also a wartime problem, particularly among the young. The incidence of syphilis among young women aged fifteen to nineteen in New York City was 204 percent higher for a ten-month period in 1944 than for the corresponding period in 1941. New York had the image of "Sin City," but problems surfaced elsewhere as well.

Terming syphilis and gonorrhea "enemy agents within our midst," reformers attacked prostitution. The May Act in 1941 allowed communities to close brothels near military establishments. By 1944, seven hundred cities had shut down their red-light districts. An internal war on vice was underway.

For all of the difficulties, the United States fared well in World War II. Almost four hundred thousand Americans were military casualties, and their loss profoundly affected families at home. By contrast, the struggle left 2.8 million German soldiers and 7.5 million Soviet soldiers dead. With civilian losses added to military figures, an estimated 20 million Russians died during the war. The United States entered the conflict late, was located far from the major battlefields, and enjoyed the benefits of prosperity within its own borders. By the middle of the conflict, nearly seven out of ten people in the United States said they had not had to make any "real sacrifices" as a result of the war.

Confident and committed, Americans were willing to do their part as they accepted the challenge they faced. Secure in their mission, they felt that their efforts would make the world a better place. They believed in their approach—successful once again—and in their destiny as they did what was necessary to support the national effort in the war. They grumbled about shortages and endured deprivations, yet even as they put up with inconveniences, they knew that conditions were far better than they had been a decade earlier. Discomforts could be tolerated with the knowledge that one day the war would end. Of course, there were some exceptions; minorities in particular had a more difficult time. But for most home-front Americans, World War II was an experience that changed their lives in positive ways.

THREE

Outsiders and Ethnic Groups

Not all Americans fared well in the Second World War. The conflict often brought difficulties for groups outside the mainstream of American life. For some, the war finally resulted in new opportunities for employment and integration; for others, it caused serious disruptions that were hard to overcome. Women, long relegated to inferior positions in the work force, now found better jobs in record numbers, though they still experienced discrimination on assorted fronts. Likewise, blacks seized on the enormous industrial expansion and pressed for upgrading to better positions. Yet they too encountered tension, as change came slowly and only in response to constant pressure on those in charge. While other minority groups benefited from the war as well, they were less well organized and enjoyed less conspicuous success. And for one ethnic group—the Japanese Americans—the war proved to be a dismal experience, unmatched by that of other ethnic or racial groups in the history of the United States.

All outsiders sensed the contradictions in a war fought for freedom and democracy by a nation that permitted discrimination at home. Propaganda portrayed the war in idealistic terms that rang untrue to those still waiting to enjoy the benefits of the coveted American dream. Thus, outsiders protested the gap between the nation's pronouncements and its practices, and used military needs to press for improvement in their lot.

WOMEN AND THE WAR

The war brought enormous changes in women's lives. Women were without question second-class citizens at the start of the struggle. They were particularly conscious of discrimination in the labor market. Numerous jobs were simply closed to women, which led to a concentration in retail trade and domestic service. In those jobs they did hold, women were usually paid less than men. During the Great Depression, conditions worsened as wives hoping to work found themselves confronting men who resented their competition.

The huge productive effort that began in 1940 opened the way to women for other forms of work. Historians have long been aware of women's influx into the work force during the war, but only recently have scholars like Susan M. Hartmann (*The Home Front and Beyond: American Women in the 1940s,* 1982) and Karen Anderson (*Wartime Women*) described in detail how the process unfolded. Initially, industrial jobs remained closed to women. Unconvinced that supplies of male labor would be depleted, employers were reluctant to modify their hiring practices. They also questioned whether women had the physical strength or mechanical ability to handle industrial tasks. The War Department supported them with the assertion that defense firms "should not be encouraged to utilize women on a large scale until all available male labor in the area has first been employed."

The situation changed as millions of men entered the military services. From late 1942 on, both government and industry waged a courtship campaign to persuade women to work. The War Manpower Commission recruited women in areas where labor was scarce. The Office of War Information issued media appeals aimed at involving women. The message stressed exciting work for good wages in a patriotic cause. An advertisement in Seattle noted that "an American homemaker with the strength and ability to run a house and raise a family . . . has the strength and ability to take her place in a vital War industry." A Baltimore ad told women that war work was "a lot more exciting than polishing the family furniture."

Women were eager to respond. The number working rose from 14,600,000 in 1941 to 19,370,000 in 1944. In the latter year, 37 percent of all adult women were in the labor force. Since some women stopped working—even as aggregate totals grew—almost 50 percent of all women were employed *at some point* during that year. At the peak of the industrial effort, women constituted 36 percent of the civilian work force.

The demographic composition shifted. The most significant change, according to William Chafe in his path-breaking account, *The American Woman: Her Changing Social, Economic, and Political Roles, 1920–1970* (1972), came among married women. Traditionally, working women had been single and young. Between 1940 and 1944, married women accounted for 72.2 percent of the total increase; thus, for the first time in American history, they outnumbered single women in the female labor force. Women with absent husbands were twice as likely as others to work; half of all servicemen's wives were employed. Older women too began to work more, as more than two million women over the age of thirty-five found jobs. By the end of the war, half of all female workers were over thirty-five.

Even more significant were the changes in the positions open to women. All kinds of new opportunities became available, the largest shift being the move out of domestic service and into manufacturing. Between 1940 and 1944, the number of women in manufacturing rose 141 percent; their share of manufacturing positions increased from 22 percent to 32.7 percent. Women were particularly active in the defense industries. In Detroit, Ford and other automobile companies finally agreed to hire women for production work. By February 1943, women made up 90.8 percent of the new workers hired in 185 war plants in that city. Elsewhere, they entered shipyard production work; by 1943, they filled 10 percent of those jobs. Women also served as steelworkers, riveters, welders, and surface miners.

Employers were glad to have the women. They believed that in certain welding tasks women could squeeze into tight places more easily than men. They assumed that women were better at repetitious and monotonous jobs than men. When hiring women, employers still kept them from most managerial posts.

But the opportunities in so many new areas were there. Over and above manufacturing positions, women's share of government jobs increased from 19.4 percent to 38.4 percent between 1940 and 1944. Several hundred thousand served in the women's divisions of the military services, where they achieved regular status (rank) and participated in all activities but combat. They worked for newspapers and radio stations in increasing numbers. Orchestra positions became available. So too did positions on the stock exchange. In countless areas, the war made a major difference in women's work opportunities.

Men were not always comfortable with the changes they saw taking place. They feared that the war would undermine femininity and breed a new class of masculine women. Columnist Max Lerner voiced his concern that the war was developing a "new Amazon" who would "outdrink, outswear, and outswagger the men." When measures were pending to create women's service divisions, opponents revealed the nature of the threat they perceived. "What has become of the manhood of America, that we have to call on our women to do what has ever been the duty of men?" one asked. A Marine Corps officer, when informed that women were being sent to his camp, was even more blunt. "Goddamn it all. First they send us dogs. Now it's women," he was said to have exploded.

Basically, opponents of women's advances were concerned about the disruption of the traditional social and sexual order, where men worked and women stayed at home. If women worked, who would take their places in seeing that everything else got done? "Who will do the cooking, the washing, the mending, the humble homey tasks to which every woman has devoted herself; who will rear and nurture the children. . . ?" one legislator asked.

The fear about children reflected a real problem. More than half a million women with children under age ten found jobs, but day-care facilities were in short supply. Official policy told women: "Now, as in peacetime, a mother's primary duty is to her home and children." The Children's Bureau declared that group care for children under two would cause "slower mental development, social ineptness, weakened initiative, and damage to the child's capacity . . . to form satisfactory relationships." But the War Manpower Commission, concerned about labor shortages, insisted that employers not discriminate against women with children, that women should be free to decide for themselves if they wanted to work. And so women worked, even as they continued to do traditional household chores and care for their children at the same time.

Women themselves shared some of the fears men voiced. They worried about their children as they arranged whatever alternatives they could. They also worried about their own femininity in their new places of work. The media helped ease women's fears. Newspaper accounts, magazine stories, advertisements, and posters all portrayed women as glamorous employees as they pursued their patriotic tasks; they could be simultaneously gorgeous and productive. Grease-stained overalls need not hide the "real woman" underneath.

Everywhere, Alan Clive ("Women Workers in World War II: Michigan as a Test Case," *Labor History,* 1979) has argued, the story was the same. Every woman riveting at the N. A. Woodworth Company looked "like a cross between a campus queen and a Hollywood starlet," according to an article in the *Detroit News*. A *McCall's* magazine story about women workers told readers: "You'll like this girl. She does a man's work in the ground crew, servicing airplanes, but she hasn't lost any of her feminine sweetness and charm." *Life* magazine featured Boeing employee Marguerite Kershner, and noted in a caption that "although Marguerite looks like a Hollywood conception of a factory girl, she and thousands like her are doing hard, vital work." The pictures of "Rosie the Riveter" underscored the theme that beauty need not be lost in the accomplishment of vital tasks. Rosie, in all forms, became a national heroine to men and women alike.

Women, for the most part, were delighted to be employed. Financial considerations played a large part in their eagerness to work. Wives of servicemen suffered losses in income when their husbands went away, and jobs helped them make up the difference as well as ease the loneliness of separation. Many women, like Josephine McKee, a mother of nine who worked at the Boeing Aircraft Company in Seattle, used war jobs to pay off debts acquired in bleaker times. Others, like Leola Houghland, a welder at Associated Shipyards (also in Seattle), used their earnings to pay for the family home. A number of women interviewed by the Women's Bureau noted that illness or disability of other family members required them to work.

Even women who had no choice but to work were pleased with the improved opportunities. Evelyn Knight left her job as a cook to work in a navy yard because: "After all, I've got to keep body and soul together, and I'd rather earn a living this way than to cook over a hot stove." Even when jobs were monotonous and routine, they were more attractive—and better paying—than those women had held before.

Countless women found paid employment a welcome respite from keeping house. One working mother noted that the "companionship of working with others is vastly more stimulating and rewarding than housework" as she recalled the "narrowing effect that staying at home full time exerts upon my outlook in life." A

Detroit government secretary declared, "[I] would just die if I had to stay home and keep house." Freda Philbrick, working at the Puget Sound Navy Yard, pointed out that "somehow the kitchen lacks the glamour of a bustling shipyard." One woman who remained at home observed of those who did not, "Some just love their jobs. I think they for the first time in their life feel important."

Patriotic considerations played an obvious part in women's willingness to work. They derived satisfaction from being able to do their part in the war. One rubber plant employee commented, "Every time I test a batch of rubber, I know it's going to help bring my three sons home quicker." Josephine Bucklin, a bus driver in Seattle acknowledged, "We do feel we're doing something concrete for the war effort." There was also an excitement, Bucklin noted, in doing "something women have never been allowed to do before."

Women felt an eagerness to prove they could do whatever was necessary. Adele Erenberg, a Los Angeles cosmetics clerk when the war started, went to work in a machine shop. Her first experience in the noisy room was intimidating, and two weeks passed before anyone spoke to her. Her response was: "Okay, you bastards, I'm going to prove to you I can do anything you can do, and maybe better than some of you." And she did.

For all of the excitement, there was frequent frustration as well. Women constantly faced the kind of cold welcome Erenberg received—particularly in jobs formerly held only by men—and simply had to wait for attitudes to change. Women also chafed under restrictions imposed by managers who were concerned about the mixing of the sexes in their plants. General Motors fired any male supervisor and female employee found "fraternizing." The company argued that questionable conduct by either party could hurt labor-management relations and compromise the policy of hiring women. Unions too imposed restrictions on women. Flint Local 599 of the United Automobile Workers voted that committeemen should ignore the grievances of any women "indecent in her wearing apparel or actions."

Worse still was the frustration that came from unfair pay differentials. Although the National War Labor Board ruled in the fall of 1942 that women who did "work of the same quality and quantity" as that of men should receive equal pay, the policy was not always fully implemented. Employers often assigned women to the lowest paying jobs in the plants. Since women had less seniority, managers could advance them more slowly and pay them correspondingly less. Moreover, managers continued to classify jobs as "men's" and "women's," with women's being paid at lower rates.

Simple figures tell the story. In the automobile industry in 1943, women averaged $44.91 per week, while men, working 3.5 hours more than women, averaged $62.65. At the Ford Willow Run plant, women in the spring of 1945 earned $2,928 annually, compared to $3,363 for men.

Still, some gains were made. Support for the principle of fairness grew in different quarters. The National Association of Manufacturers endorsed the idea of equal pay. Industries proved cooperative when cost-plus contracts allowed them to pay women more at no expense to themselves. Unions pressed for equal pay when women directly replaced men, although they failed to challenge discrimination when men and women worked in different jobs. By early 1944, the NWLB had heard from more than twenty-two hundred companies that had eliminated discriminatory differentials. Disparities between the average earnings of men and women narrowed somewhat during the war, but the basic problem remained.

For all of their involvement in the work force, Susan M. Hartmann has suggested in *The Home Front and Beyond,* women remained committed to traditional values during the war. Though they took advantage of new opportunities, they continued to feel as strong a commitment to marriage and family as before. The marriage rate rose, at least until the draft depleted the male population. Between 1940 and 1943, there were 1,118,000 more marriages than would have been expected before that time. The number of children aged five and under increased by 25 percent. Popular culture continued to stress the woman as wife and mother before all else.

Yet women flourished in their new positions, and many wanted to continue working after the war. Surveys taken between 1943 and 1945 revealed that from 61 percent to 85 percent of the women working wanted to stay employed. For married women, the positive sentiments ran from 47 percent to 68 percent.

Women were not without ambivalence. While many women may have enjoyed their experience in the work force, they recognized the pressures that would make it hard for them to stay on. As one woman who worked for the Naval Advance Depot in Tacoma noted: "My husband wants a wife, not a career woman." Others, however, either needed to continue in their jobs for financial reasons or simply wanted to hold on to what they had gained. That desire came squarely into conflict with the wish of servicemen to return to former positions when they came home, and to restore the patterns of life they remembered from before the war.

Just as industrialists and government officials had campaigned earlier to draw women into war plants, they campaigned to encourage them to leave their jobs when the struggle ended. The federal government emphasized that wartime work was temporary. Betty Allie, a Michigan unemployment official, noted: "When the period of postwar adjustment comes, and their men come home . . . you will see women returning naturally to their homes." Jane Stokes, speaking on the radio for her union in the aircraft industry, declared: "When this war is over—I'll get a manicure, put on the frilliest dress I can find, pour a whole bottle of cologne over my head, and THEN, I'll be GLAD to give up my Union chair in the Eagle Airie Room to some boy who comes marching home deserving it."

As demobilization took place, women found themselves released from factory jobs at almost double the rate for men. In the summer of 1945, three-fourths of the women in the shipbuilding and aircraft industries were let go; shipbuilding became a male bastion once again. The female share of jobs in the Detroit automobile industry fell from 25 percent to 7.5 percent. The positions available to women in all areas were often less attractive and lower paying than those open to men.

World War II undoubtedly had an important effect on women's lives. William Chafe (*The American Woman*) underscored the changes that occurred, but subsequent feminist scholars like Susan Hartmann (*The Home Front and Beyond*) and Karen Anderson (*Wartime Women*) have focused on the ephemeral nature of the changes and have argued that the appeal to women's patriotism led them to work for national ends rather than personal satisfaction, thereby dampening aspirations when the fighting was over.

Even though wartime gains were lost and progress thwarted in the postwar period, significant changes had occurred. The struggle had led to improvements in women's lot, and the behavioral shifts that took place helped foster attitudinal shifts that provided the groundwork for a women's movement in later years. Thus, World War II was an important step on the road to equal rights.

THE BLACK STRUGGLE FOR EQUAL RIGHTS

So too did the Second World War help promote the cause of equality for American blacks. A movement aimed at ending discrimination against blacks had been underway since the early years of the twentieth century, but blacks remained acutely aware of the gap between American dream and American reality in the United States. In the South, the Jim Crow system, which mandated rigid separation of the races, was firmly entrenched. Though segregation was less legally binding in the North, residential patterns, with blacks congregating in urban ghettoes and slums, yielded the same result. Organizations like the National Association for the Advancement of Colored People (NAACP) protested racist conditions and sought to chip away at the framework of segregation, but progress was slow.

There had been only minimal change in the decades before World War II. Though blacks had supported the American effort in the First World War, they had discovered in the aftermath little inclination on the part of government or the public to support them in their struggle for equal rights. The New Deal held out hope for change, but blacks found that with its other political priorities, the administration did little for them as a separate group. The only gains came from programs that assisted the poor in general.

At the start of World War II, blacks faced discrimination on a variety of fronts. Unemployment remained high—one of every five workers lacked a job—and good jobs were even harder to obtain. The U.S. Employment Service continued to accept employers' requests for "whites only," thus perpetuating existing discriminatory patterns. In 1940, only 240 of the 100,000 workers in the aircraft industry were black. The jobs that blacks did find open frequently involved unskilled dirty work at low pay. Blacks worked most often in positions such as janitors, bellhops, or garage attendants. Black women were even worse off, with prejudice toward them more entrenched than that directed at black men.

The situation was little better in the military services. Blacks were not allowed to join the Air Corps or Marine Corps. In the Navy, they could enlist only in the all-black messmen's branch; in the Army, they were segregated from whites and confined to the few regular black units created after the Civil War. Humiliations accompanied the military service that was permitted. Blacks were resentful when the Army, like the Red Cross, separated blood plasma according to the donor's race. They were bothered too by the slights they encountered when stationed in the South. Lloyd Brown recalled being turned away from a lunchroom in Salina, Kansas, only to see German prisoners of war being served at the counter. "This was really happening," he exclaimed. "It was no jive talk. The people of Salina would serve these enemy soldiers and turn away black American GIs."

Many Americans denied that any problems existed. A poll in 1942 revealed that six out of ten whites felt that blacks were comfortable with the way things were and deserved no further opportunities. A majority believed that blacks' inferior social status was due to personal shortcomings and not to white resistance to change.

Prejudice was strongest in the South, where members of the South Carolina House of Representatives asserted their "allegiance" to white supremacy as they pledged their lives and their "sacred honor" to maintain the system. But acceptance of traditional patterns was strong even in other parts of the country. In the West and Northeast, whites, when interviewed, voiced their approval of separate schools, restaurants, and neighborhoods.

Popular attitudes were mirrored within the administration. Secretary of War Stimson had strong views on the question of race. The crusty old Republican viewed blacks as inferior, for they had scored lower than whites on World War I intelligence tests. Though the tests measured educational achievement rather than intelligence, Stimson's mind was set; blacks were unfit for advancement. "Leadership," he said, "is not embedded in the negro race yet and to try to make commissioned officers to lead men into battle—colored men—is only to work disaster to both." General George C. Marshall, a Virginian responsible for organizing the massive Army effort at home, agreed. Desegregation, he felt, would destroy morale.

Franklin Roosevelt was more concerned with military questions than minority rights. The "integrity of our nation and our war aims is at stake in our attitude toward minority groups at home," he acknowledged, but he was reluctant to engage in long-range future planning. "I don't think, quite frankly," he said at the end of 1943, "that we can bring about the millenium at this time."

Yet a movement for change was underway. Richard M. Dalfiume ("The Forgotten Years of the Negro Revolution," *Journal of American History,* 1968) was one of the first to point to the roots of postwar reform in the war period itself; and Neil A. Wynn (*The Afro-American and the Second World War,* 1976) later provided the fullest and best-documented account of black experience during the war.

Pressures came in part from the contrast between professed ideals and actual practice in the United States, particularly in a war against a fascist foe. Blacks charged that Jim Crow restrictions approximated the racist regulations of the Nazis. Noting the paradox, one soldier writing to FDR stated that the Army, the "very instrument which our government has organized and built . . . to fight for world democracy, is within itself undemocratic."

Pressures came too from the force of numbers. Like whites, blacks gravitated toward industrial centers in search of work, though the black migration lagged behind the white movement and was, in the end, less massive than it had been in World War I. Still, some seven hundred thousand blacks crossed state lines during the Second World War, four hundred thousand of them leaving the South. Between 1940 and 1946, the black population in San Francisco grew 560 percent, compared to a 28.1 percent white increase. In Los Angeles, black growth was 109 percent compared to 17.7 percent for whites. In Detroit's Willow Run area, black growth was 47 percent compared to 5.2 percent for whites. Concentration only exacerbated discontents.

Blacks became more assertive as they launched their own two-pronged attack. The *Pittsburgh Courier,* a widely circulated black newspaper, proclaimed a "Double V" campaign—V for victory in the war against the dictators overseas, V for victory in the struggle for fair treatment at home. Blacks "would be less than men," the *Courier* suggested, "if, while we are giving up our property and sacrificing our lives, we do not agitate, contend, and demand those rights guaranteed to all free men . . . this would be neither patriotism nor common sense." Blacks wanted something more from the war than the wry epitaph that originated during the period: "Here lies a black man killed fighting a yellow man for the protection of a white man."

One thing they particularly wanted was the chance for full military participation. If blacks could fight alongside whites, Richard M. Dalfiume (*Desegregation of the United States Armed Forces: Fighting on Two Fronts, 1939–1953,* 1969) has observed, they could expect the rights and privileges of full American citizenship as well. As the *Crisis,* the publication of the NAACP, declared: "This is no fight merely to wear a uniform. This is a struggle for status, a struggle to take democracy off of parchment and give it life." Black spokesmen pressured legislative and executive leaders even before Pearl Harbor, and their efforts brought the promotion of Colonel Benjamin O. Davis to the rank of general—the first such appointment in American history. They also managed to change policy so that blacks were eligible for general service in the Navy and Marine Corps, though still on a segregated basis. The Army, in need of manpower, accepted more and more blacks—the number rose from 97,725 in November 1941 to 467,883 in December 1942. The proportion of blacks in the Army, however, still lagged behind the proportion in the general population, and the Army too remained segregated.

Black pressures began to coalesce in January 1941, when A. Philip Randolph, head of the Brotherhood of Sleeping Car Porters, proposed a massive March on Washington under the slogan: "WE LOYAL NEGRO AMERICAN CITIZENS DEMAND THE RIGHT TO WORK AND FIGHT FOR OUR COUNTRY." Randolph, as Jervis Anderson (*A. Philip Randolph: A Biographical Portrait,* 1973) has shown, was a firm believer in the use of power. "The Administration leaders in Washington," he declared, "will never give the Negro justice until they see masses—ten, twenty, fifty thousand Negroes on the White House lawn!" He wanted a "thundering march" that would "shake up white America."

The March on Washington Movement sought to exclude whites on the premise that blacks had to fight for their own rights if they wanted to make progress. In advocating that blacks work to attain their own ends, Randolph wanted to "create faith by Negroes in Negroes." The movement also sought to mobilize the masses rather than the middle class, and it underscored the need for direct action on an unprecedented scale, rather than quiet negotiation and compromise.

When Randolph met with the president in mid-June 1941, he presented a series of demands, including an end to discrimination in employment; an end to discrimination and segregation in the federal government; and an end to discrimination and segregation in the armed forces. Roosevelt was worried about the possibility of violence in Washington, a city with southern values and customs, and had already attempted to head off the march with expressions of support for equal opportunity. Meeting Randolph face-to-face, the president tried to use his well-known powers of persuasion to get Randolph to back off, but the black leader pressed for "something concrete, something tangible." They finally agreed that a committee would draft an executive order that met with Randolph's approval.

A week later Roosevelt signed Executive Order 8802, declaring "that there shall be no discrimination in the employment of workers in defense industries or government because of race, creed, color, or national origin." To implement the policy, he created a Fair Employment Practices Committee (FEPC) to investigate complaints and take appropriate action. In response, Randolph called off the march.

The FEPC was never wholly effective. It was underfunded and understaffed from the start. Initially made up of six part-time members and a small staff, it had a budget of but $80,000 in the first year. It began operations in the Office of Production Management, moved to the War Production Board, and a year after its creation found itself in the War Manpower Commission. But change of location seldom brought improvement in its ability to fulfill its responsibilities.

The FEPC's powers were severely circumscribed. It was a temporary war agency dealing solely with defense industries. Furthermore, it could only act against discrimination when formal complaints were made. And even when discrimination was evident and proof forthcoming, the agency lacked the authority to enforce its recommendations. It had to rely on publicity and persuasion to facilitate change.

Concerned more with production than promotion of equality, the president remained aloof. But in mid-1943, as manpower needs became more pressing, he moved the FEPC to the Executive Office. With a new location and new leadership, a larger budget and increased authority to conduct investigations, the agency became more aggressive. Chairman Malcolm Ross was aware of both its limitations and possibilities. "We may not be able to wipe out discrimination overnight," he said, "but where war manpower needs are at stake we can and shall try."

The FEPC enjoyed a few notable successes. In the summer of 1944, after it directed that blacks be upgraded to positions as streetcar operators in Philadelphia, a public transportation strike paralyzed the city. With war production involved, the government responded immediately. The Army assigned soldiers to transit vehicles, the FBI arrested strikers, and the selective service system warned that it would draft employees who did not return to work. The strike, as Allan M. Winkler ("The Philadelphia Transit Strike of 1944," *Journal of American History,* 1972) has observed, ended in victory for the forces favoring racial equality, but only because military needs were threatened, thus leading the government to act.

On balance, the accomplishments of the FEPC were limited. The agency successfully resolved only one-third of the eight thousand complaints it received, and but one-fifth of those coming from the South. Employers or unions ignored or defied thirty-five of forty-five compliance orders issued. Yet, as one War Manpower Commission official noted, the FEPC did keep the issue of fair treatment alive: "It forced people to look, day after day, at this problem of the Negro's economic handicaps."

And improvements did occur, particularly after 1943. When the U.S. Employment Service ceased honoring requests that specified race and the National Labor Relations Board refused to certify unions that excluded minority membership, the way cleared for easier black access to the work force. Between April 1940 and April 1944, the number of blacks employed rose from 4.4 million to 5.3 million, with most of the gains coming in the latter years. In 1942, blacks comprised 3 percent of all war workers; in 1945, the figure had risen to 8 percent. The federal government itself increased the number of black employees from sixty thousand to two hundred thousand.

Meanwhile, blacks pressed for change on other fronts. The NAACP and the Urban League continued to work in traditional ways: publicizing grievances, exerting political pressure, and using the courts. Other blacks, following Randolph's example and recognizing that militancy was necessary, began to take nonviolent direct action in pursuit of racial equality. The Committee on Racial Equality (CORE), founded by pacifists in 1942, was a biracial organization that began to demonstrate against segregation in a number of cities. In Baltimore, Chicago, Denver, and Detroit, CORE members conducted sit-ins at a number of movie theaters and restaurants and achieved their goal: an end to segregation in these public places.

Their example mobilized black students at Howard University in Washington, D.C. In the spring of 1944, a number of them entered Thompson's, a segregated restaurant located where black government workers could have enjoyed access. Outside, other students picketed with signs reading: "Are you for Hitler's Way or the American Way? Make Up Your Mind" and "We Die Together. Let's Eat Together." In time, their persistence paid off and helped lead to the easing of segregation in some parts of the capital city.

Despite modest progress, racial problems persisted throughout the war. The migration of blacks and whites into urban centers of war production strained housing and transportation facilities. Blacks found their housing choices limited, and therefore concentrated in ghetto areas that became strained to the breaking point. In areas of San Francisco formerly inhabited by the Japanese, 10,000 people lived where 5,000 had been before. In Chicago, 300,000 blacks crowded into the South Side in a region thought able to hold a maximum of 225,000.

Detroit too was terribly overcrowded. By 1943, half of the black families there lived in substandard homes. The year before, the city faced a serious struggle over the Sojourner Truth housing project, built for blacks, then demanded by whites to ease overcrowding they too felt. Black protests ensured that the complex was designated for blacks, but not without ill feeling on both sides. Tensions were growing all the time. In August 1942, *Life* magazine published a story entitled "Detroit Is Dynamite," and concluded that "Detroit can either blow up Hitler or it can blow up the U.S."

The explosion, described by Harvard Sitkoff in "The Detroit

Race Riot of 1943" (*Michigan History,* 1969), came on a Sunday evening in June 1943, in the midst of a heat wave. One hundred thousand people, 85 percent of them black, congregated in Belle Island Park, a recreation area near the black ghetto of Paradise Valley. Scuffles between blacks and whites in early evening led to more serious violence. Rumors of rape and murder spread. The most common story was that whites had thrown a black woman and her baby off a bridge. Before long, a full-scale race riot was underway. Blacks looted and destroyed white-owned stores. Whites pulled blacks out of theaters and off streetcars and beat them. The police stood by and did little, save for shooting some looters. By the time the riot was over several days later, 25 blacks and 9 whites were dead, 675 people were injured, and about $2 million of property had been destroyed.

In New York City's Harlem, another uprising, described by Dominic J. Capeci (*The Harlem Riot of 1943,* 1977), took place at the beginning of August. When a rumor spread that a policeman had killed a black soldier, the community erupted. Sweeping through the business district, blacks smashed windows, entered stores, and carried away goods. Though no battles between blacks and whites took place, 6 blacks were killed and 300 injured. The Harlem uprising reflected the same frustrations and resentments that erupted in Detroit and surfaced in other cities throughout the nation.

To what degree did the war bring lasting change for blacks? Without question, it broke down barriers that had held them back in the past. Increased access to the military services and to industrial positions made a difference. So did the Supreme Court's decision abolishing the white primary election in 1944. At the same time, such modest gains may, in fact, have had the effect of dampening racial militancy, as Harvard Sitkoff has asserted in challenging those scholars who have seen the war as a watershed. Blacks remained disadvantaged, politically, socially, and economically, though a start toward greater equality had been made. But further change was necessary, and an explosive force was building that could not forever be contained. As Walter White, head of the

NAACP, wrote: "A wind *is* rising—a wind of determination by the havenots of the world to share the benefits of freedom and prosperity which the haves of the world have tried to keep exclusively for themselves. . . . Whether that wind develops into a hurricane is a decision we must make."

HISPANICS AND THE WAR

Like women and blacks, Hispanics faced discrimination during World War II. In 1940, about 1.5 million Spanish-speaking people lived in the United States. Some concentrated in eastern cities; many more lived in the West and Southwest. Chicanos— Mexican Americans—were the most numerous of all. Often invisible in standard treatments of World War II, only recently have Hispanic Americans begun to receive adequate attention in monographs and history texts. Rodolfo Acuña (*Occupied America: A History of Chicanos,* 1981) has provided the most comprehensive account of Chicanos during the war years as well as other times. Chicanos, he has shown, often found themselves grouped together with blacks and separated from whites by skin color. Moreover, they had to deal with the additional disadvantage of speaking a foreign language. "For Coloreds and Mexicans," a sign outside a Texas church read. Deprived of adequate jobs, they frequently settled in run-down areas. Lacking political influence, they found it difficult to break the poverty cycle.

Wartime manpower shortages helped Chicanos just as they helped other groups. When military personnel were necessary, the government drafted 350,000 Mexican Americans into the armed forces. Mexican-American farm workers, like other rural Americans, gravitated to the cities in search of better jobs; their migration was part of a trend that had begun in the 1920s.

The war brought significant changes in what had been a largely unskilled, agricultural labor force. Anticipating future manpower needs, between 1939 and 1942 the Department of Labor's Office of Education established vocational schools in cities like Albuquerque and Sante Fe, New Mexico, and Las Vegas, Nevada. The schools provided rural Americans with training as plumbers, mechanics, and welders, and eased the transition into war work.

Chicanos made striking gains. In 1941, no Mexican American was employed in the Los Angeles shipyards; by 1944, 17,000 worked there. They also worked in shipyards and aircraft factories in Seattle, Long Beach, Corpus Christi and Albuquerque. Some headed for other major war production cities: Detroit, Chicago, Kansas City, and New York.

At the same time, changes in agricultural hiring took place. When the war caused an acute farm labor shortage, the United States looked to Mexico for aid. Faced with the problem of providing food for both the home front and the military, American growers sought to import Mexicans to work in the fields. Initially, the growers wanted simply to open the border and hire at the lowest possible rate, but they were forced to capitulate when Mexico insisted on contracts guaranteeing basic rights. An agreement in 1942 providing for transportation, food, shelter, and medical care led to the entrance of several hundred thousand *braceros* (helping arms) over the next few years.

Despite protective agreements and new jobs, Mexicans and Mexican Americans continued to suffer discrimination in the United States. *Braceros* grumbled about withheld wages and miserable working conditions. Industrial employees often found themselves passed over when available supervisory or skilled jobs went to whites. And, like women, they sometimes received lower wages for the same work as that done by white males.

Chicano tensions, like black frustrations, were most visible in the crowded cities. Some young Mexican Americans, uncomfortable in white society, roamed the streets in groups or gangs. Known as *pachucos,* they favored a distinctive costume—the zoot suit—consisting of trousers flared at the knees but tighter at the ankles, a loosely cut coat reaching to mid-thigh, a long key chain, and a felt hat. It set the wearer apart and frightened middle-class Americans, who associated the zoot suit with gang activity and violence.

The atmosphere in Los Angeles, where many Chicanos lived, was volatile. Newspapers abetted fears with charges of Mexican crime. A city council ordinance prohibited the wearing of zoot suits. Police units roamed through East Los Angeles and made sudden searches. Then, in August 1942, a young Mexican was found lying on a dirt road near the Sleepy Lagoon just outside the city; he died without regaining consciousness. Charging foul play, the police used the corpse as an excuse to round up twenty-two gang members and beat confessions from them. Two asked for a separate trial and hired good legal help; charges against them were dropped. In a travesty of justice only later reversed, twelve of the others were convicted of murder, five were convicted of manslaughter, and three were placed on probation.

An even worse episode occurred in early June 1943, when sailors based in Los Angeles sought revenge on Chicanos who had allegedly attacked them as the sailors searched for women. Rampaging through the streets, the sailors stormed into bars and movie theaters, seized *pachucos,* and tore zoot suits from people's bodies. Both military and civilian law enforcement officials either stood aside or arrested Chicanos without cause; the press only fanned the flames. Eventually, naval personnel were ordered out and the riot came to an end, but it left a surge of anger in its wake.

NATIVE AMERICANS
AND THE WAR EFFORT

American Indians in the United States also became actively involved in the war effort. Their treatment in the past 150 years, Commissioner of Indian Affairs John Collier observed in "The Indian in a Wartime Nation" (*The Annals of the American Academy of Political and Social Science,* 1942), "could hardly be expected to produce loyal citizens devoted to the Nation's welfare and willing to defend it against its enemies." Yet Indians, like members of other minority groups, sensed the larger stakes of the struggle and willingly offered their military and industrial support.

Though native Americans in three states were denied the right to vote, they were still subject to the draft; thus, approximately twenty-five thousand served in all branches of the military, most of them in the Army. Indians from tribes with a warrior tradition proved especially willing to enlist. The Mission Indian Federation of California sent "a message of loyalty and readiness to serve our great Nation." The Crow tribe of Montana enthusiastically offered the government all of its manpower.

Indians served well in combat and other capacities. Ira Hayes, a Pima from Arizona, received extensive media coverage as one of three survivors at Mount Suribachi on Iwo Jima where Marines, after fighting a heroic and legendary battle, managed to raise the American flag. Some Navajos worked as code talkers; their language was so rare that it served as a secret means for transmitting Marine Corps messages by radio and phone.

Indians in the military still met with discrimination. On occasion, they were limited to clerical duty or support work behind the lines. Where there was only one Indian in a unit, that man often found himself called "Chief." Stereotypes remained intact. Nonetheless, military service went smoothly and many Native Americans were decorated for their heroic deeds.

Indians made a substantial home-front contribution as well. Nearly fifty thousand worked in war industries throughout the country. Two thousand Navajos helped build a sizable ordnance depot in New Mexico. Other Indians constructed aircraft on the West Coast and all kinds of military materials in the major war production centers.

The war hastened the process of detribalization, thus accelerating native-American assimilation into the larger society. As thousands left their reservations for military or industrial jobs, they had to make rapid adjustments to mainstream America. When the war ended, Indians serving abroad or moving to other parts of the nation were less likely to settle back into older patterns. Some made the transition easily; others felt a sense of alienation and rootlessness. All were faced with a lifestyle change that could not simply be ignored.

ITALIAN AMERICANS UNDER ATTACK

Some ethnic or racial groups had especially severe problems that were unique to the war. Those from nations with which the United States was fighting had the worst time. German Americans, who had been treated poorly in the First World War, were now more fully assimilated into American life and thus left alone. Italians and Japanese found themselves targeted this time.

For Italian Americans, conditions in the United States were harsh and grim. As more recent arrivals, most of the nearly five million living in the United States were immigrants or children of immigrants. In 1942, six hundred thousand of them still were not naturalized. Uneducated and unskilled, they often had trouble finding jobs. Unassimilated, they felt like outsiders in their new home. Many, John P. Diggins has argued in *Mussolini and Fascism: The View from America* (1972), looked with pride and affection on Benito Mussolini and the "New Italy." As Paul Pisicano, a resident of an Italian-speaking neighborhood during the war, later recalled, "Mussolini was a hero, a superhero. He made us feel special, especially the southerners, Sicilian, Calabrian."

Italian Americans, caught between two cultures, had lived in an uneasy peace until the onset of the war. In June 1940, Franklin Roosevelt aroused apprehension when he condemned Mussolini for his "stab in the back" of France. A wave of suspicion swept the country as anti-Italian sentiment became more pronounced than ever before. An executive order the day after Pearl Harbor designated noncitizen Italians enemy aliens. Those affected found physical movement and employment opportunities limited.

Stung by the stigma and resentful at what they felt was unfair discrimination, Italian Americans worked to have the designation changed. They finally succeeded on Columbus Day, in October 1942, when the government reversed its policy in formal recognition of the loyalty Italian Americans had shown. Now naturalization procedures were simplified. Highly visible Italian Americans like baseball player Joe DiMaggio were hailed as the new heroes. The assimilation of this group into American society was underway.

JAPANESE AMERICANS: CIVILIAN CASUALTIES OF WAR

Japanese Americans were less fortunate than other ethnic groups. Historians have long been documenting the extreme discrimination they faced. Morton Grodzins (*Americans Betrayed: Politics and the Japanese Evacuation,* 1949) was one of the early critics of Japanese-American treatment during the Second World War. Later, Roger Daniels (*Concentration Camps U.S.A.: Japanese Americans and World War II,* 1971) provided a vivid description of the difficulties encountered. Most recently, Peter Irons (*Justice at War,* 1983) has dissected the Justice Department's decision-making process which, combined with other factors, led to the forced relocation—and internment—of the Japanese. The government's claim that it had to act on military grounds has been debunked in the literature on the affair.

Japanese Americans suffered for being a tiny minority from a nation with which America was at war. Though only 127,000—roughly one-tenth of 1 percent of the U.S. population—lived in America at the start of the war, they were visible and vulnerable. Some 47,000 Issei—Japanese born abroad—were ineligible for naturalization by the Immigration Act of 1924. About 80,000 Nisei—Japanese Americans born in the United States—and Sansei—their children—enjoyed citizenship, yet most were concentrated on the West Coast where prejudice, stemming from irritation at their willingness to take low-paying jobs, had existed for years. The attack on Pearl Harbor gave nativist groups, who had long sought Japanese exclusion, their chance. As one Native Son of the Golden West declared, "This is our time to get things done that we have been trying to get done for a quarter of a century."

Anti-Japanese sentiment intensified in the early months of the war. Shocked by what had happened at Pearl Harbor, Americans were prepared to believe anything and to act accordingly. Hostile signs were seen everywhere. Rumors, all of them untrue, spread about West Coast sabotage. A barbershop in California offered "free shaves for Japs" but said it was "not responsible for accidents." *Time* and *Life* magazines told readers how to tell friendly Chinese from enemy Japanese: "The Chinese expression is likely to be more placid, kindly, open; the Japanese more positive, dogmatic, arrogant." There were other differences, too: "Japanese walk stiffly erect . . . Chinese more relaxed . . . sometimes shuffle." Government officials contributed to the attacks on Japanese living in the United States. "A Jap's a Jap," said General John DeWitt, head of the Western Defense Command. "It makes no difference whether he is an American citizen or not. . . . I don't want any of them." The governor of Idaho was even more explicit: "A good solution to the Jap problem would be to send them all back to Japan, then sink the island. They live like rats, breed like rats, and act like rats." Even liberal journalist Walter Lippmann added his voice to those favoring internment.

Faced with growing political and public pressure, the Army cited military necessity to justify its decision to evacuate all West Coast Japanese. Executive Order 9066, signed by the president in mid-February 1942, referred to all enemy aliens, but was applied only to the Japanese—citizens and noncitizens alike. When evacuation began and it became clear that other parts of the country were unwilling to accept the Japanese, the Army shifted course. A newly created War Relocation Authority (WRA), acting with presidential and congressional approval, brushed constitutional niceties aside and moved 110,000 Japanese Americans to ten camps in seven western states. Milton Eisenhower, General Dwight D. Eisenhower's brother, served as first head of the agency. He hoped the camps could perform useful projects and thereby transform the mood of the country from bitterness to tolerance toward the Japanese; he soon realized how naive that hope was. The hatred for Japanese Americans persisted through the end of the war.

The camps, located in desolate areas and protected by barbed wire and armed guards, contained wooden barracks covered by tar paper; the barracks were divided into one-room apartments. Each room, shared by a family or unrelated group, had in it only cots, blankets, and a light bulb. Toilet, laundry, dining, and bathing facilities were communal. In those cramped quarters, traditional relationships broke down. Older Japanese found their authority questioned by the younger Nisei who could better handle daily difficulties. Social cohesion was shattered. Some Japanese became seriously depressed.

By 1943, the WRA had developed a system of removing from the camps those Japanese who showed no evidence of disloyalty and could find jobs elsewhere in the nation. By the end of 1944, the agency had allowed thirty-five thousand internees, mostly Nisei, to leave. Trouble arose, however, when the War Department tried to register evacuees for military service, and 28 percent of the male Nisei refused to renounce their allegiance to the emperor of Japan. The government's response was to segregate further 18,500 disloyal Japanese in Tule Lake, California, in quarters that were even worse than the original camps.

Finally, in early 1945, the administration chose to let all Japanese leave the camps. Some, who had found their only security in the strained quarters, were reluctant to go, but again had no choice. At first, they received some help in relocating, but soon the WRA left them on their own.

The entire experience was the worst violation of civil liberties in wartime America. In addition to psychological trauma, the Japanese suffered $400 million in income and property losses. Yet the U.S. Supreme Court upheld the evacuation of the Japanese in several court cases in 1944. Though authorities later acknowledged they had gone too far, the fact remains that Japanese Americans were civilian casualties of the war.

Outsiders fared differently than other Americans in the Second World War. Some used military and industrial demands to agitate for change and alter the circumstances of their lives. Women and blacks in particular made substantial gains on the labor front, gains that opened the way and provided the model for future reform. Hispanic Americans and native Americans sought to apply the same kind of pressure, but they were less numerous and less organized and therefore enjoyed fewer gains. Their quest for equality waited a later time.

Yet Hispanics and Indians were still better off than the unassimilated groups who were the real American victims of the war. Just as the refrain "military necessity" helped some citizens, it hurt others, particularly immigrants from enemy nations. As millions of Americans enjoyed better times, others experienced hardships—not of their own making—they could not overcome. For them, the war brought burdens, not benefits, and revealed the limitations of the American dream.

FOUR

The Politics
of War

The political sphere grew increasingly contentious during World War II. While consensus and solidarity in the struggle against the Axis powers remained intact from beginning to end, there was growing polarization over domestic issues. The political world has always reflected the major issues of the day, and electoral contests have long served to articulate a culture's values and views. The major wartime elections—presidential and congressional—revolved around the concerns Americans felt as they responded to military and industrial demands, concerns about wages, prices, shortages, and the very process of mobilization itself. These elections recorded the debates on how home-front priorities should be set and revealed the disagreements about what the nature of the postwar world should be. Political maneuvering, a part of the governing process at all levels, focused on issues that could not be ignored and delineated the boundaries of American society as it dealt with the experience of war.

During the Second World War, the United States became increasingly conservative at home. Republicans and southern Democrats, who had begun to resist what they considered the encroachments of the New Deal even before the start of the war, now found the way clear to effect the cutbacks they sought. The administration, dependent on bipartisan support on other fronts, was unwilling to resist their efforts, particularly given the return of prosperity. Consequently, though inequities remained, further reform had to wait.

Yet the Roosevelt coalition, created in 1936 and described most fully by Samuel Lubell in *The Future of American Politics* (1951), stayed intact. Comprised largely of urban, ethnic members of the working class, it continued to be a powerful force in American political life, even as pluralities declined. Although the coalition faced constant challenge and underwent continuous change, it stuck together in the presidential election years. It was less successful, however, in the midterm contests when FDR was not running.

THE ELECTIONS OF 1940 AND 1942

Franklin Roosevelt, still the dominant political force in 1940, sought an unprecedented third term. At that time, the nation, having just begun to enjoy the first fruits of recovery from the depression, started to worry about the European war. The conflict, which began in 1939, gave rise to growing concern the next year as Adolf Hitler overran western Europe. In mid-1940, France fell to the Axis powers while the plight of Great Britain became more and more desperate. As Americans began providing overseas aid, they became progressively aware of the possibility of formal U.S. involvement. Thus, Roosevelt, who had dreamed of retiring and returning to his home in Hyde Park, New York, felt he had no choice but to run again.

The Republicans nominated Wendell L. Willkie, a business executive who was a dark horse but ran a brilliant nominating campaign. President of the Commonwealth and Southern Utilities Corporation, Willkie had come to believe that the New Deal had gone too far—even though he had voted Democratic most of his life. *Time, Look,* and other magazines touted him; two thousand Willkie clubs supported him; at the convention itself, his supporters chanted "We Want Willkie" even when no business was being conducted. When the balloting began, Willkie's momentum prevailed and he won the nomination.

In the general campaign, the Republicans criticized the centralizing tendencies of the New Deal and its inability to achieve recovery. The New Deal threatened individualism and free enterprise, Willkie charged, and destroyed private initiative. "Only the productive can be strong, and only the strong can be free," he declared. Though Willkie at first supported the administration's foreign policy initiatives, he claimed that the harassment and restriction of business had undermined defense efforts by leaving the nation unable to protect itself. Roosevelt countered by pointing to defense preparations already underway and to the economic gains those efforts were bringing. Inspection tours of defense plants and military installations drew attention to the positive results.

As he continued to lag behind the president, Willkie sharpened his attack. Seizing upon Americanism as an issue, he charged that dictatorship was possible if Roosevelt gained a third term. Another victory for FDR would violate a sacred principle of government, Willkie alleged, and could only result in a totalitarian end. Willkie also shifted course on defense. Eager to gain the support of his party's isolationist wing, he argued that Roosevelt intended to lead the nation into war.

Roosevelt responded in a series of blistering speeches aimed at convincing anxious Americans of his dedication to peace. He sought to reassure ethnic groups like the Irish, Italians, and Germans, who feared the United States would align itself with the British against the Axis. Underscoring his intention of keeping the nation out of war, he proclaimed: "I have said this before, but I shall say it again and again and again: Your boys are not going to be sent into any foreign wars." When it was pointed out that the nation might be attacked and he might not be able to keep his promise, FDR retorted that in case of attack it would no longer be a foreign war.

In the end, the election turned on FDR. Though his opponents still cringed at the thought of "that man," after eight years in office Roosevelt remained overwhelmingly popular with laborers and other low-income voters, who credited him with the return of prosperity that they were beginning to feel. Roosevelt won 55 percent of the popular vote and gained a 334 to 197 vote victory in the electoral college. His five-million vote margin was considerably smaller than his eleven-million vote plurality in the 1936 election, but it was still enough for a clear-cut win. Once again, as John W. Jeffries has demonstrated in his sophisticated quantitative analysis, *Testing the Roosevelt Coalition: Connecticut Society and Politics in the Era of World War II* (1979), FDR's strength came in the cities from foreign-stock, working-class groups who kept the New Deal coalition alive. In the 1940 congressional contests, the Democratic party gained slightly in the House but the Republicans picked up five seats in the Senate. Still, the Democrats retained control of both chambers with sizable majorities.

The Democrats had a tougher time in 1942. In the midterm elections, they confronted a growing conservative coalition that really came into its own during the war.

That opposition group had been on the rise for five years. According to James T. Patterson (*Congressional Conservatism and the New Deal: The Growth of the Conservative Coalition in Congress, 1933–1939,* 1967), it began to coalesce as early as 1937, when rural elements of FDR's constituency objected to proposals aimed at assisting northern industrial groups. The president's effort to pack the Supreme Court provided his opponents with a ready-made issue, and from that time on Republicans and southern Democrats banded together to resist any perceived encroachments on their philosophical turf. This meant they blocked administration initiatives on all but international or war-related questions.

The war intensified various groups' resistance to Roosevelt. Farmers favoring high food prices grumbled about price controls aimed at checking inflation for consumers around the country. Southerners complained when worker shortages extended greater employment opportunities to blacks and talked of bolting the Democratic party. Republicans pointed to inefficiency in the war mobilization effort and to the adverse effects of mobilization on constituent groups. While "Congress cannot assume to run the war," Republican Senator Robert A. Taft acknowledged, "it does have the job of reasonable criticism." Taft and his colleagues were intent on making sure their voices were heard.

The resistance became clearly visible in 1942, when people who were prosperous once more could afford to forget the assistance the Democrats had given them in the past. With the war not yet going particularly well militarily, there seemed to be cause for complaint.

Republicans made substantial inroads in the 1942 congressional elections. They gained 44 seats in the House, giving them a total of 209—only 13 fewer than the Democrats' 222—and 9 seats in the Senate. Low voter turnout made a significant difference in the final results; only twenty-eight million people voted in 1942, compared to fifty million in 1940. Republican turnout remained relatively stable. The Democratic party—with far more draft-age voters, and relocated war workers who had not yet met residency requirements—suffered most of all.

The Republicans knew what they wanted. As *Fortune* magazine observed:

The victorious candidates rode an anti-Roosevelt and an anti-Washington wave. They were almost entirely normalcy men, quiet, churchgoing, family men, not quite prohibitionists, men whose outlook was limited to their states and their regions. They may be relied upon to investigate Washington thoroughly. Many of them think they have a mandate to repeal all New Deal reforms.

Compounding the effect of the Republican gains was the increased strength of Democrats from the South; Democratic defeats in the North and Midwest enhanced southern influence. In the House, representatives from fifteen southern and border states claimed 120 of the 222 Democratic seats; in the Senate they held 29 of 57 seats. They also dominated the major committees. Thus, when Republicans and southern Democrats banded together, they constituted an almost insurmountable bloc.

THE ELECTION OF 1944

Despite the 1942 congressional challenge, the president remained politically strong two years later. Physically, however, he had deteriorated. An attack of influenza at the end of 1943 left him debilitated and weak. A general physical examination several months later revealed (according to his personal physician) that FDR suffered from "hypertension, hypertensive heart disease, [and] cardiac failure (left ventricular)." He found his braces— necessary for his polio-crippled legs—increasingly difficult to use, and he often appeared irritable and worn out.

Nonetheless, Roosevelt was determined to seek another term—and his renomination was never in question. But given the president's failing health, the compelling issue for the Democratic party was the selection of a vice-presidential nominee. According to John Morton Blum (*The Price of Vision: The Diary of Henry A. Wallace, 1942–1946*, 1973), Henry A. Wallace, FDR's choice in 1940, had drifted beyond the shifting consensus of American politics. The idealistic Wallace had asserted his commitment to internationalism in ringing terms. When *Life* magazine publisher Henry Luce proclaimed "the American Century"—where American might would be predominant throughout the globe—Wallace countered that "the century on which we are entering—the century which will come out of this war—can and must be the century of the common man." And he remained committed to the course of domestic reform at a time when other Americans (or at least their representatives in Congress) were willing to pause or turn back.

Roosevelt could have dictated his choice of a running mate as he had in 1940. Instead, bowing to political realities, he left the selection to the convention itself. There, after a behind-the-scenes struggle that included Alben Barkley, Senate majority leader from Kentucky, William O. Douglas, a New Dealer now on the Supreme Court, and James F. Byrnes, Roosevelt's "assistant president," Harry S Truman, senator from Missouri, emerged with the nomination. Truman was a compromise choice, acceptable to all. His Missouri background reassured the South; his ties to the notorious Pendergast machine made political bosses sympathetic; and his leadership of a Senate committee that investigated the defense program gave him liberal support.

On the Republican front, Governor Thomas E. Dewey of New York was the leading candidate. After making his reputation by prosecuting underworld figures, Dewey proceeded to forge an impressive record as governor. Although he had revamped the state's fiscal system, improved the workmen's compensation system, and arranged for low-income housing subsidies—all reform measures—he argued that the New Deal had gone too far. "It is absolutely necessary that we get rid of the New Deal to save the country," he declared in 1940.

Dewey won the nomination, but his age and personality were liabilities that did not endear him to voters. At forty-two he seemed too young to be president. Moreover, he appeared arrogant, stiff, and dull. "How can we be expected to vote for a man who looks like the bridegroom on a wedding cake?" Alice Roosevelt Longworth asked. "Smile, Governor," a photographer once said. "I thought I was," Dewey replied. Critics claimed he suffered from "intellectual halitosis," and declared he was a man "who could strut sitting down."

In the 1944 campaign, both candidates responded to voters' desires for postwar prosperity and peace. Both endorsed some kind of international organization that could help promote future stability as internationalism came of age; and both tried to provide assurance of domestic stability in the years ahead. The possibility of postwar unemployment was a pressing public concern. The war had brought an end to the trials of the Great Depression. Would the nation revert back to pre-1940 conditions when the struggle was over? In industrial states like Connecticut where nine out of ten workers were engaged in war production, unemployment fears were particularly pronounced. Roosevelt and Dewey agreed that the government had a responsibility to guarantee the availability of jobs.

The Democrats took advantage of their close ties with labor. Hoping for a large working-class turnout, as two out of three union members called themselves Democrats, they launched massive drives to register new voters. A thousand Democratic workers convassed Detroit; in St. Louis, their counterparts registered 36,000 people in a single day. The AFL and CIO cooperated in working for FDR, and the CIO established a Political Action Committee (PAC) to promote Democratic candidates who were sympathetic to labor. The PAC gave organized labor a flexibility that Congress had tried to curtail in the Smith-Connally Act; it raised money, distributed literature, and made sure voters got to the polls. The basic approach was traditional, but the scale of operation was new.

The Republican campaign, which proved dull at the start, soon became venomous. Once again, the Republicans used the Americanism issue, but this time they went far beyond their 1940 charges. Now they seized on the menace of communism, which they linked with the Democrats and FDR. "Insidious and ominous are the forces of Communism linked with ir-religion that are worming their way into our national life," declared vice-presidential nominee John Bricker. "These forces are attempting to take a strangle hold on our nation through the control of the New Deal." Republicans pointed to CIO-PAC leader Sidney Hillman's alleged communist sympathies and claimed that Roosevelt had told Democrats to "clear everything with Sidney." PAC really stood for "Party of American Communism," said Clare Booth

Luce in her campaign for reelection to Congress from Connecticut.

Republicans also engaged in personal attacks on FDR. Dewey himself called the president "old and tired." Others circulated rumors about his health and charged that he was dying of diseases ranging from cancer to syphilis. Newspaperman Drew Pearson accused Roosevelt of sending a Navy destroyer back to the Aleutian Islands, at taxpayers' expense, to retrieve his little dog, Fala, who had been left behind.

The president fought back. The campaign, described most vividly by James MacGregor Burns (*Roosevelt: The Soldier of Freedom*, 1970), seemed to revive FDR, to make him animated again. At a banquet given by labor officials in September, he demonstrated that he had lost none of his political punch. In his speech, broadcast nationwide over radio, he disposed of the health issue with the acknowledgment that since the last campaign, "I am actually four years older, which is a fact that seems to an-*noy some* people." As he defended his record and lit into the Republicans, his deadpan delivery and mock seriousness brought laughs and cheers. And then he came to the question of his dog: "These Republican leaders have not been content with attacks— on me, or my wife, or on my sons. No, not content with that, they now include my little dog, Fala. Well, of course, I don't resent attacks, and my family doesn't resent attacks, but Fala *does* resent them. I am accustomed to hearing malicious falsehoods about myself—such as that old, worm-eaten chestnut that I have represented myself as indispensable," he went on. "But I think I have a right to resent, to object to libellous statements about my dog."

In the balloting, Roosevelt won again. His plurality—3.6 million votes—and his share of the popular vote—53.4 percent—both were down from 1940, but he still emerged with an overwhelming 432 to 99 vote victory in the electoral college. The urban vote made the difference. In cities larger than one hundred thousand, Roosevelt received nearly 61 percent of the vote. He won a number of states—New York, New Jersey, and Pennsylvania, among others—because his plurality in the largest city was greater than the Republican majority in other parts of the state. Thus, the Democratic coalition remained intact, albeit with minor modifications. FDR lost some support among white Southerners but continued to draw strength from the workers, ethnic Americans, and city dwellers who had elected him in the past.

In the congressional elections, the results were mixed. The Democrats won twenty-two seats in the House, as the urban vote proved decisive in enabling them to regain Republican seats. In the Senate, the Democrats lost one seat. In neither chamber did the outcome dramatically alter the Republican-southern Democratic coalition. That coalition proved dominant in the legislative sphere, where it had the power to exert its will on the domestic front from the beginning of the war to the end, presidential victories notwithstanding.

THE CONSERVATIVE COALITION

Roosevelt knew the nature of the opposition and tried to respond accordingly. He understood that the process of domestic reform had run its course in the 1930s. He understood too that he had to make concessions to the coalition in the interest of support for his military conduct of the war. In a press conference at the end of 1943, he declared that the New Deal had come when the patient—the United States—was suffering from a grave internal disorder. But then, at Pearl Harbor, the patient had been in a terrible external crash. "Old Dr. New Deal," the president said, "didn't know 'nothing' about legs and arms. He knew a great deal about internal medicine, but nothing about surgery. So he got his partner, who was an orthopedic surgeon, Dr. Win-the-War, to take care of this fellow who had been in this bad accident."

Roosevelt's acknowledgment of political reality made little difference in the outcome of legislative contests. The coalition of Republicans and southern Democrats, strong throughout the war, came into play in four of every ten close Senate votes in 1944. Conservatives, as Richard N. Chapman (*Contours of Public Policy, 1939–1945,* 1981) has shown in a systematic numerical analysis, had both the inclination and the ability to change the domestic agenda in ways they had long sought. "It is no longer feared, it is assumed," Archibald MacLeish noted, "that the country is headed back to normalcy, that Harding is just around the corner, that the twenties will repeat themselves."

The conservative coalition left its mark on the home front. Arguing that the New Deal had gone too far and that misguided reform efforts had needlessly interfered with individual initiative in the economic realm, the coalition moved to roll back whatever programs it could. Its members wanted to cut back what they considered the inflated size of government, to circumscribe the power of labor, and to end planning schemes that they contended went too far. They succeeded in virtually every sphere.

The first attacks on the New Deal came in 1942. The Civilian Conservation Corps (CCC) had long been one of the more popular agencies. Concerned with conservation of forest and water resources, the CCC had undertaken some noteworthy projects in addition to putting people back to work. But even though the agency participated in the defense effort by training enrollees to read blueprints and perform other tasks useful to the military, by 1942 its mandate had run its course and its numbers began to decline. Public opinion no longer supported continuing the conservation camps. Roosevelt himself, despite a personal fondness for the CCC, suggested that it might remain useful for boys below draft age "for only very nominal purposes, such as looking after parks, historic places, and forests." Congress was unwilling to go even that far and provided only enough money for the orderly liquidation of the agency.

So it was with the Works Progress Administration (WPA). Work relief had made a real difference in the darkest days of the depression, but conditions were different now. Like the CCC, the WPA faced numerical decline as better jobs became available in the massive war production effort. Two-thirds of those on WPA rolls left in the year following Pearl Harbor. Political opponents, long opposed to the boondoggles they claimed the agency funded, clamored for its dissolution. WPA supporters remained silent. "I'll bet half the people who were on W.P.A. wouldn't admit that fact if they were asked," one Democrat said. Recognizing the handwriting on the wall, Roosevelt gave the WPA an "honorable discharge" at the end of 1942. The last relief payment came a few months later.

In 1943, the National Youth Administration (NYA) became another wartime casualty. It had survived the year before because it had provided vocational training in skills useful to the defense industries, and because businessmen, who appreciated the way it brought potential recruits to a central location, had spoken in its defense. But when worker shortages required the hiring of untrained workers, the NYA's purpose was undermined. Now critics had the upper hand. Southerners, who objected to the recruitment and training of black workers, argued for the agency's demise. Education officials, perceiving the NYA as a competitor, charged that its existence was the first step toward federal control of education and advised Congress to "kill this octopus before it kills us." Congress obliged by abolishing the agency.

Congress also killed the National Resources Planning Board (NRPB) in 1943. Engaged in formulating plans and assessing priorities for the postwar period, the NRPB, in several pamphlets issued in 1942 and 1943, proposed the expansion of social services and social security coverage for the needy and impoverished. It also called for public works projects to stimulate the economy when such projects became necessary to promote full employment. Opponents, who had long frowned on any such planning, resisted those suggestions. This was socialism, the president of the National Association of Manufacturers declared. Congress cut off funding for the NRPB and left it with only enough money to conclude its affairs.

Other agencies suffered a similar fate. The Farm Security Administration, which had helped low-income farmers buy land and machinery and thus produce more, found its budget slashed in 1942 and 1943, and was left with barely enough to limp along. The Rural Electrification Administration, a source of irritation to private power companies, was cut back as well.

Even wartime organizations had to face the wrath of Congress. The Office of War Information, America's propaganda agency, alienated Republicans in particular, who charged that the goal of the Domestic Branch was primarily to obtain a fourth term for FDR. Early in 1943, Senator Rufus C. Holman of Oregon came across the first issue of the OWI publication *Victory* which contained an article on Roosevelt, who was pictured against the background of the American flag. Holman objected to the story which characterized the president as a kindly man whose philosophy ran counter to "the toryism of the conservative reactionary." The whole magazine, he said, was but "window dressing" for another Roosevelt campaign. At budget time, all OWI opponents joined forces. Representative John Taber of New York called OWI "a haven of refuge for the derelicts" and Representative Joe Starnes of Alabama termed domestic propaganda "a stench to the nostrils of a democratic people." Thus, the Domestic Branch was severely circumscribed.

The same pattern held with other legislation; reform proposals stood little chance of passage. For example, the 1943 Wagner-Murray-Dingell bill, which would have expanded the social security system by extending coverage and increasing benefits, was defeated. There was also trouble over taxation, as John Morton Blum has shown in detail in *From the Morgenthau Diaries*.

The effort to raise money sparked a sharp confrontation between the executive and legislative branches. New revenue was necessary to support the war effort. Though the Treasury Department sought $12 billion in 1943, Roosevelt himself insisted that the request be pared down to $10.5 billion. With the election of 1944 looming, Congress was unwilling to raise taxes and passed a bill providing only $2 billion, a bill that also made substantial tax concessions to business interests.

Furious at the limited revenue the bill provided and at its inequities, Roosevelt sent an angry veto message to Capitol Hill in February 1944. The measure, he said, was "wholly ineffective" for meeting national needs. With its "undefensible privileges for special groups," he went on, "it is not a tax bill but a tax relief bill providing relief not for the needy but for the greedy."

Congress responded in kind. Democratic majority leader Alben Barkley, a longtime supporter of FDR, voiced his personal irritation at the president and resigned, calling the veto message "a calculated and deliberate assault upon the legislative integrity of every member of Congress." He called on his colleagues to override the veto. They did, by overwhelming margins, and Senate Democrats reelected Barkley leader as well.

On two counts Roosevelt had met a stinging defeat at the hands of an intransigent Congress. First, the measure was inadequate for its intended purposes. Second, it was the first revenue act ever passed over a presidential veto. It was but one more indication of the strength of the conservative coalition in national affairs.

Roosevelt met with defeat after defeat on domestic questions. He found himself constantly hemmed in either by military demands or by political constraints stemming from congressional unwillingness to support him in anything but the war effort.

So it was with reconversion. The real question as the war neared an end was when civilian production could be resumed. Business leaders were anxious to retool as quickly as they could in order to be ready to supply the market that had been waiting for scarce goods. Military leaders objected, asserting that to shift course away from military production would diminish a sense of urgency at home and compromise home-front morale.

When the Allied advance following the D-Day landings on June 6, 1944, slowed down, Roosevelt recognized that he had little latitude to buck the military. Therefore, he eased out Donald Nelson, head of the War Production Board, who had been clamoring for reconversion. In this episode, as in so many others, the president had no choice but to accept the constraints he faced.

EXECUTIVE LEADERSHIP AND EXPANSION

Though Roosevelt was frequently disappointed at the direction public policy took on the home front, he understood that wartime needs came first. Committed to victory first and foremost in a two-front war, he needed both military and congressional support for his overseas efforts and thus had to accept compromises on domestic questions. Even so, he did whatever he could to keep a liberal agenda alive.

In early 1944, drawing on the proposition of the by then defunct National Resources Planning Board that the postwar government should guarantee economic as well as political rights, FDR staked out his position. In his State of the Union message, he called for enactment of "a *second Bill of Rights* under which a new basis of security and prosperity can be established for all." He sought a commitment to provide useful jobs and adequate wages in addition to decent housing, education, and protection from the ravages of old age, illness, accident, or unemployment. "*All* of these rights spell security," he declared. "And after this war is won," he continued, "we must be *prepared* to move *forward,* in the implementation of these rights, to new goals of happiness and well-being."

The Economic Bill of Rights, rooted in the reforms of the New Deal, had little chance to pass, but it did express FDR's hope that his administration's past efforts could be renewed when the war was won. Roosevelt wanted to keep the country looking ahead, whatever the actions of Congress, and he repeated his proposals throughout 1944. "We are not going to turn the clock back!" he said. "We are going forward."

Taking the first step toward implementing his vision, the president proposed extending generous benefits to the one group Congress could not deny—the veterans of the war. He first suggested the idea in the autumn of 1943, then let it proceed in a form recommended by the American Legion, a politically influential veterans' organization, early the next year. His effort, detailed by Keith Olson in *The G.I. Bill, the Veterans and the Colleges* (1974) was successful. The Servicemen's Readjustment Act—the GI Bill—provided liberal unemployment benefits, gave veterans preference in finding jobs, offered them substantial educational assistance (in the form of tuition payments and living supplements), and guaranteed loans for the purchase of a small business, farm, or home. In short, it underscored the commitment to security and prosperity that was so much a part of the American dream.

Though Congress increasingly asserted its own prerogatives,

wartime leadership came from the White House. Roosevelt understood the need to provide direction, and in response to that need, the office of the presidency enjoyed continued growth. The power of the president had been expanding since the first days of the New Deal. Roosevelt had acted more aggressively than any of his predecessors: He had delivered messages, provided drafts of bills, and given direction as the legislative process unfolded. The proliferation of alphabet agencies—the NRA, PWA, WPA, CCC, and TVA, to mention but a few—was a testament to the ever more active executive role. In 1939, as Richard Polenberg (*Reorganizing Roosevelt's Government: The Controversy over Executive Reorganization, 1936–1939,* 1966) has noted, FDR regularized the changes that had taken place with the creation of the Executive Office, which included the Bureau of the Budget and other agencies that could assist in providing executive direction. Administrative channels and important agencies were now more firmly under control. The Executive Office provided the mechanism for later expansion of the executive branch and gave Roosevelt the authority to move as he saw fit.

The war brought even further growth; the entire federal government expanded astronomically. Between 1940 and 1945, the number of civilian employees rose from 1 million to 3.8 million, with much of the expansion found in the executive branch. The president assumed sweeping powers which he delegated to the various war agencies. Under the umbrella of the Office of Emergency Management, a whole series of new agencies attempted to meet the demands of defense and war mobilization. Administrative organization had been makeshift in the past. By the middle of the war, a new structure was in place. A pattern in which people became accustomed to looking to Washington for answers was established that continued after the war.

Roosevelt insisted on a position of dominance during the war, and within the areas he perceived as most important, he got his way. Historians and other scholars have been increasingly aware of how much presidential power grew as a result of the war in Vietnam and the Watergate affair. Arthur M. Schlesinger, Jr., in *The Imperial Presidency* (1973), has shown clearly that much of that growth was rooted in the New Deal and World War II years. As commander in chief, Roosevelt took responsibility for making the necessary military decisions and for participating in all diplomatic discussions throughout the war. Yet he was equally insistent on the need to maintain power on important questions at home.

In the autumn of 1942, when Congress seemed tempted to balk at price control legislation, FDR asserted his constitutional position. "In the event that the Congress should fail to act, and act adequately, I shall accept the responsibility, and I will act," he said. "The President has the powers, under the Constitution and under congressional acts, to take measures necessary to avert a disaster which would interfere with the winning of the war." Even former President Herbert Hoover agreed with the general principle. "To win total war President Roosevelt must have many dictatorial economic powers," he said. "There must be no hesitation in giving them to him and upholding him in them." Despite charges of dictatorship, FDR got his way on the price control issue.

Roosevelt's position was not possible in every case, he understood, and Congress had to be accorded latitude in other areas, whatever his views. But FDR was prepared to insist on his leadership rights when in his judgment the war hung in the balance. After the struggle, powers he had assumed could be channeled elsewhere.

The Supreme Court upheld the president's position. It approved price controls and the actions taken to relocate the Japanese. It also rejected cases arising from the seizure of war plants. Clearly, strong executive action was not questioned during the struggle.

HARRY S TRUMAN

Though Franklin Roosevelt was undeniably the dominant American leader in World War II, he failed to see the fighting come to a successful end. On April 12, 1945, the ailments that had been plaguing him in recent years finally caught up with him. While relaxing at Warm Springs, Georgia, he suffered a massive cerebral hemorrhage and within minutes he was dead.

And so, in the final months of the war, political leadership fell to another man. Harry Truman, little known outside the Senate, now tried to step into Roosevelt's shoes. It was an awesome task. "Who the hell is Harry Truman?" Admiral William D. Leahy had asked when informed the year before of the choice of the vice-presidential nominee. Other Americans wondered the same thing. Those who knew were not always pleased. "That Throttlebottom Truman," TVA director David Lilienthal called him during the transition.

Truman, as Cabell Phillips (*The Truman Presidency: The History of a Triumphant Succession,* 1966) and Robert J. Donovan (*Conflict and Crisis: The Presidency of Harry S Truman, 1945–1948,* 1977) have shown in sympathetic treatments, was not particularly well-prepared for his new job. Roosevelt had never taken him into his confidence, and Truman, as he assumed power, was therefore poorly informed on the major issues he faced. He felt painfully inadequate at the start. "I don't know whether you fellows ever had a load of hay fall on you," he told reporters the day after he became president, "but when they told me yesterday what had happened, I felt like the moon, the stars and all the planets had fallen on me." To a former Senate colleague he admitted, "I'm not big enough. I'm not big enough for this job." David Lilienthal agreed. "The country," he said, "doesn't deserve to be left this way."

Yet Truman soon became more comfortable in his new position. He was a feisty politician who responded to the challenge he faced. Unlike Roosevelt, he was impulsive. He was eager to act, to take matters into his own hands. A sign on his White House desk read, "The Buck Stops Here." Under Secretary of State Joseph C. Grew was delighted with Truman's brisk manner. "When I saw him today," Grew wrote in the month after Truman assumed command, "I had fourteen problems to take up with him and got through them in less than fifteen minutes with a clear directive on every one of them. You can imagine what a joy it is to deal with a man like that."

Truman faced a number of major issues that required difficult decisions. He had to decide how the new atomic bombs would be used. He had to determine how enemy surrender could best be achieved, and how Allied cooperation could be maintained. And he was responsible for carrying through with the politically volatile domestic agenda inherited from Franklin Roosevelt.

From the moment he took office, Truman was intent on following Roosevelt's lead. As the war drew to an end, his messages asserted the same governmental responsibility for the maintenance of economic security that FDR had proclaimed. The Fair Deal, foreshadowed in those early days, followed the example of the New Deal. The political difficulties it encountered on the home front were the same ones that had developed during the war.

Politics, as ever, reflected American priorities in World War II. Basic social values surfaced in all the legislative and electoral contests that occurred and the spectrum of home-front attitudes was visible in political debate. Americans longed for peace and prosperity throughout the struggle, though they disagreed on the means to achieve their ends. Their disagreements caused domestic policy to shift course as they defined new boundaries in public affairs.

CONCLUSION

Without question, the Second World War changed American society, but just how much? Historians, particularly in recent years, have argued about the degree of the war's impact, and have tried to determine just what the war brought that was new. The contrast between changes sparked by the war and continuities with developments in past years is not always one that can be clearly and crisply drawn, but it provides a starting point in the attempt to understand the ultimate effect of the war. Richard Polenberg, in *War and Society,* Geoffrey Perrett in *Days of Sadness, Years of*

Triumph, and James MacGregor Burns, in *Roosevelt: The Soldier of Freedom,* are among those who have stressed the importance of the changes that made the United States undeniably different after the war than it had been before.

The nation, in that analysis, had suffered no physical destruction. There had been no bombing raids within continental borders, no battles on American shores. Yet the highly orchestrated involvement in the greatest struggle ever known had brought economic, social, and political change to an unprecedented degree.

The war ushered in the Keynesian revolution as it brought a return of prosperity after the dismal days of depression in the 1930s. The massive spending that began in 1940 provided the best possible demonstration of the positive steps that could be taken to mitigate the effects of a business cycle that seemed stalled on a downward turn: aggressive public policy *could* make a difference. The way was now clear for experimentation with fiscal policy to avoid economic crisis in the years ahead.

World War II promoted the growth of big business, as it underscored the military-industrial links that made possible the massive production necessary for the war. War Department ties with the nation's largest firms remained important even after the struggle was over. Similarly, the war contributed to the development of organized labor, which became less militant but more firmly entrenched in the industrial marketplace, and thus more influential in the bargaining over wages and working conditions that took place. The nation's largest farmers also became more powerful than they had been before.

The war brought demographic change. The migrations toward war production centers created population shifts that affected the postwar geographic balance. Cities in the West and the South received a boost that spurred their development. The baby boom that accompanied the return of servicemen affected the development of all American institutions.

For many American "outsiders," the war was a vehicle for social and employment gains. Though social reform gave way to other demands as the United States pursued a necessitarian approach to the struggle, women and blacks especially were able to insist on changes when their own interests coincided with larger military demands. The need for labor, as the draft drew workers into the armed forces, opened new opportunities for groups outside the mainstream of American life. Thus, the war proved to be a stimulus—and a model—for future change.

The war changed political relationships and patterns. Americans now looked to the government as never before; administrative choices made during the struggle affected subsequent events. Decisions to build war plants in certain locations and not others determined the nature of future industrial development. Housing built in wartime continued to be used, of course, in later years. The government had played the dominant role in all cases, and even when private initiative became more important, people still sought guidance and direction from Washington.

The presidency grew even more powerful than it had been. Faced with the most pressing demands any chief executive had ever encountered, Franklin Roosevelt proved willing to experiment and act, just as he had a decade earlier. His active approach in military and diplomatic affairs, his acceptance of the need to create new agencies to meet mobilization demands, and his willingness to take whatever executive action was necessary were all factors that contributed to the expansion of the presidential role. Although contractions occurred in the postwar years, the basic patterns forged during the war endured.

The war gave a boost to the conservative coalition of southern Democrats and Republicans that had begun to form in the late 1930s. Even as the president assumed more power, Congress demanded a voice and played an influential part in home-front affairs. The New Deal had provided the reform agenda in the 1930s. The conservative coalition in Congress defined what reform was and was not possible in the war and postwar years.

And yet, as John Morton Blum, in *V Was for Victory,* and John W. Jeffries, in *Testing the Roosevelt Coalition,* have argued, it would be a serious mistake to see developments of the war period in terms of change alone. Continuity with the past was important, and basic American values endured. As Americans looked ahead, they did so through the perspective of the past. They remained attached to the status quo as they sought to create a more attractive, stable, and secure past.

Most Americans, whether in the military or at home, wanted to win the war and then return to the patterns they remembered. They hungered for the prosperity they recalled from the 1920s, so elusive in the 1930s, now once again possible. Their vision for the future included no brave and bold new world, but a revived and refurbished version of the world they had known before. The war restored the self-confidence they had felt prior to the depression and convinced them that what they wanted was within their grasp. The American dream, its contours the same, remained alive and well.

The changes that unfolded were not always the dramatic shifts they first appeared to be. Many were rooted in trends that had been unfolding for years, even decades, in the United States. For example, business had been developing rapidly throughout the post–Civil War period. Wartime changes were simply part of a larger pattern. The military-industrial complex did not begin with World War II. Many of the same ties and connections can be seen in the mobilization for the First World War.

The list of past ties goes on and on. The process of labor organization was rooted in the 1930s when perhaps the greatest shifts occurred. And wartime migrations were nothing new: World War I had seen similar movement, particularly among blacks who headed north for the first time. Basic political patterns stayed remarkably stable during the war, with the Roosevelt coalition surviving as the dominant force in electoral life.

Other shifts, the argument goes, were similarly less substantial than they initially appeared. Though blacks pressed for reform and sowed the seeds for the postwar civil rights movement, they remained disadvantaged and discriminated against during the war. They were still denied equal access to the armed forces, and even as they took jobs previously denied them, they had to accept employment restrictions. Women too made significant gains, yet they faced discrimination in their new positions. As women improved their economic status, they continued to see themselves—

and be seen by society—in their traditional roles as wives and mothers; and when the war was over, they found themselves pressured to return to those roles.

Continuities and limitations notwithstanding, the changes that took place between 1940 and 1945 cannot be denied. Seen against a broader perspective, the changes the United States experienced were profound. Military requirements and production demands resulted in significant social and economic shifts. Responding to the challenges it faced, the United States was different at the end of the war than it had been at the start. In area after area, the patterns of the postwar period were established.

Some of the changes were liberal; some were not. Business concentration and centralization made for greater efficiency but posed a threat to the independent entrepreneur and the ordinary American, both concerned with personal well-being and advancement in a world where economic mobility was slowly being choked off. Reforms in the composition of the work force, on the other hand, meant more positive results for the "little man." The incremental gains provided a sense of new possibilities and contributed to momentum that grew in later years.

War, by its very nature, has always been a catalyst for change, and the Second World War was no exception. In democracies and dictatorships alike, major change took place. In the United States, World War II made Americans more willing to involve themselves—politically and diplomatically—with the outside world. It also altered their hopes and expectations and the patterns of their lives at home.

Bibliographical Essay

For several decades after World War II, historians wrote extensively about the New Deal and the Cold War but neglected the wartime home front in the United States. In the 1970s and 1980s, however, that gap has begun to be filled by several comprehensive treatments and by an increasing number of specialized studies examining all aspects of the struggle.

Without question, the two best books on the period are Richard Polenberg, *War and Society: The United States, 1941–1945* (Philadelphia, 1972) and John Morton Blum, *V Was for Victory:*

Politics and American Culture During World War II (New York, 1976). Polenberg provides an evenhanded and useful assessment of the important wartime developments. Blum includes a fuller sense of the culture and its constraints in his more extended account. Also helpful to fill out the general picture are Richard R. Lingeman, *Don't You Know There's a War On? The American Home Front, 1941–1945* (New York, 1970), and Geoffrey Perrett, *Days of Sadness, Years of Triumph: The American People, 1939–1945* (New York, 1973). James L. Abrahamson has a very good chapter on World War II in *The American Home Front* (Washington, D.C., 1983). Lee Kennett, *For the Duration: The United States Goes to War, Pearl Harbor—1942* (New York, 1985), examines the first six months of the struggle. Anthologies that can be used to supplement the above works include: Richard Polenberg, ed., *America at War: The Home Front, 1941–1945* (Englewood Cliffs, N.J., 1968); Chester E. Eisinger, ed., *The 1940s: Profile of a Nation in Crisis* (Garden City, N.Y., 1969); and Keith L. Nelson, ed., *The Impact of War on American Life: The Twentieth-Century Experience* (New York, 1971).

On Franklin D. Roosevelt, such a dominant figure during the war, there is a vast literature. A number of the standard books about FDR in the early New Deal and war years give the best sense of the man. To begin, see William E. Leuchtenburg, *Franklin D. Roosevelt and the New Deal, 1932–1940* (New York, 1963); Arthur M. Schlesinger, Jr., *The Age of Roosevelt: The Coming of the New Deal* (Boston, 1958); and *The Age of Roosevelt: The Politics of Upheaval* (Boston, 1960). Equally useful are James MacGregor Burns, *Roosevelt: The Lion and the Fox* (New York, 1956), and *Roosevelt: The Soldier of Freedom* (New York, 1970). To fill out the picture with speeches and public statements, see Samuel I. Rosenman, ed., *The Public Papers and Addresses of Franklin D. Roosevelt*, X–XIII (New York, 1950).

On war mobilization and economic policy, an official account that provides a good starting point is the United States Bureau of the Budget, *The United States at War: Development and Administration of the War Program by the Federal Government* (Washington, D.C., 1946). John Morton Blum, *From the Morgenthau*

Diaries: Years of War, 1941–1945 (Boston, 1967) gives a clear overview of events from the vantage point of the secretary of the treasury. Eliot Janeway, *The Struggle for Survival* (New Haven, Conn., 1951) is a still useful description of the governmental effort. Also important is Robert Cuff, "American Mobilization for War, 1917–1945: Political Culture vs. Bureaucratic Administration," in N. F. Dreisziger, ed., *Mobilization for Total War: The Canadian, American and British Experience, 1914–1918, 1939–1945* (Waterloo, Ontario, Canada, 1981). Two helpful memoirs are: Bruce Catton, *The War Lords of Washington* (New York, 1948), and Donald Nelson, *The Arsenal of Democracy* (New York, 1946). Alan Clive, *State of War: Michigan in World War II* (Ann Arbor, Mich., 1979) gives a full description of the effects of mobilization on one state.

For the vindication of John Maynard Keynes and an assessment of war spending on U.S. economic health, see Robert Lekachman, *The Age of Keynes* (New York, 1966). On the growth of government-business ties, the most incisive assessment is Paul A. C. Koistenen, *The Military-Industrial Complex: A Historical Perspective* (New York, 1980). To study further the consequences of centralization, check the Report of the Smaller War Plants Corporation, *Economic Concentration and World War II* (Washington, D.C., 1946).

There is a full literature on more specific economic questions. Barton J. Bernstein, "The Automobile Industry and the Coming of the Second World War," *Southwestern Social Science Quarterly,* XLVII (1966) examines the conversion to a war footing. On tax policy, Randolph E. Paul, *Taxation for Prosperity* (Indianapolis, Ind., 1947) is helpful. John Kenneth Galbraith, "Reflections on Price Control," *Quarterly Journal of Economics,* LX (1949) looks at wartime price questions. For a discussion of the effort to apportion automobile fuel, see James A. Maxwell and Margaret N. Balcom, "Gasoline Rationing in the United States," *Quarterly Journal of Economics,* LX (1946). On the development of a synthetic rubber industry, see William M. Tuttle, Jr., "The Birth of an Industry: The Synthetic Rubber 'Mess' in World War II," *Technology and Culture,* 22 (1981). The best accounts of the development of the atomic bomb are: Martin J. Sherwin, *A World Destroyed: The Atomic Bomb and the Grand Alliance* (New York, 1975), and Barton J. Bernstein, "Roosevelt, Truman, and the Atomic Bomb, 1941–1945: A Reinterpretation," *Political Science Quarterly,* 90 (1975). For agricultural developments, Walter W. Wilcox, *The Farmer in the Second World War* (Ames, Iowa, 1947) is the place to begin.

A number of good studies document the important role of labor during the war. The best recent treatment is Nelson Lichtenstein, *Labor's War at Home: The CIO in World War II* (New York, 1982). Lichtenstein gives a full sense of labor developments as he describes the increasing bureaucratization of the movement. An earlier but still helpful account is Joel Seidman, *American Labor from Defense to Reconversion* (Chicago, 1953). David Brody, *Workers in Industrial America: Essays on the 20th Century Struggle* (New York, 1980) puts wartime developments into a broader perspective. Irving Bernstein, *Turbulent Years: A History of the American Worker, 1933–1941* (Boston, 1969) provides a vivid view of the background period. Two helpful volumes on the 1940s edited by Colston E. Warne are *Yearbook of American Labor* (New York, 1944), and *Labor in Postwar America* (New York, 1949). On the United Automobile Workers, see Irving Howe and B. J. Widick, *The UAW and Walter Reuther* (New York, 1949), and Martin Glaberman, *Wartime Strikes: The Struggle against the No-Strike Pledge in the UAW* (Detroit, Mich., 1980). On John L. Lewis, see both Saul Alinsky, *John L. Lewis* (New York, 1949), and Melvin Dubofsky and Warren Van Tine, *John L. Lewis: A Biography* (New York, 1978).

The question of the social impact of World War II can be pursued in a variety of different ways. Lingeman, *Don't You Know There's a War On?*, and Perrett, *Days of Sadness, Years of Triumph* both describe domestic changes and developments, from fads to favorite pastimes. Blum, too, in *V Was for Victory,* gives a sense of the wartime mood in once-again prosperous times. Clive, *State of War* gives a real feeling for the impact of war on the people of Michigan. Two older treatments that remain useful are Francis E. Merrill, *Social Problems on the Home Front* (New

York, 1948), and William F. Ogburn, ed., *American Society in Wartime* (Chicago, 1943). For a perceptive collection of essays that tells veterans about the changes that occurred in the United States, see Jack Goodman, ed., *While You Were Gone* (New York, 1946).

On more specific social issues, the literature is growing. To pursue the question of war aims, at both public and policy levels, see Blum, *V Was for Victory* and Allan M. Winkler, *The Politics of Propaganda: The Office of War Information, 1942–1945* (New Haven, Conn., 1978). For population shifts, Henry S. Shryock, Jr. and Hope T. Eldridge, "Internal Migration in Peace and War," *American Sociological Review*, XII (1947) is useful. Even more helpful on the migrations and the consequences for public policy is Philip J. Funigiello, *The Challenge to Urban Liberalism: Federal-City Relations during World War II* (Knoxville, Tenn., 1978).

Other kinds of works also help to describe American society in the war. Harriette Arnow's moving novel *The Dollmaker* (New York, 1954) vividly conveys the crowded conditions and human difficulties in wartime Detroit. Pictures can be equally important. Ronald H. Bailey and the editors of Time-Life Books have done a first-rate job of collecting photographs in *The Home Front: U.S.A.* (Alexandria, Va., 1977). Oral history, likewise, can give a feeling for the period, and two recent works are especially useful: Studs Terkel, *"The Good War": An Oral History of World War II* (New York, 1984), and Mark Jonathon Harris, Franklin D. Mitchell, and Steven J. Schechter, *The Homefront: America during World War II* (New York, 1984).

In recent years, there has been a good deal of creative work done on the status of women in World War II. The best starting point is William Chafe, *The American Woman: Her Changing Social, Economic, and Political Roles, 1920–1970* (New York, 1972). Since Chafe wrote, a number of other scholars have examined in greater detail shifting work patterns and the related question of social role. Two very useful surveys of women's wartime experience are: Karen Anderson, *Wartime Women: Sex Roles, Family Relations, and the Status of Women during World*

War II (Westport, Conn., 1981), and Susan M. Hartmann, *The Home Front and Beyond: American Women in the 1940s* (Boston, 1982). Similarly helpful are two studies by Eleanor Straub, "United States Government Policy toward Civilian Women during World War II," *Prologue,* 5 (1973), and "Government Policy toward Civilian Women during World War II," (Ph.D. dissertation, Emory University, 1973), as well as a perceptive study by D'Ann Campbell, *Women at War with America: Private Lives in a Patriotic Era* (Cambridge, Mass., 1985). See also Leila Rupp's thoughtful comparative treatment, *Mobilizing Women for War: German and American Propaganda, 1939–1945* (Princeton, N.J., 1978).

On more specific topics, there are a number of pertinent works. For women's military role, begin with the official history, Mattie E. Treadwell, *The United States Army in World War II: Volume VIII: The Women's Army Corps* (Washington, D.C., 1954). On women's employment, a still useful early book is Constance McLaughlin Green, *The Role of Women as Production Workers in War Plants in the Connecticut Valley* (Northampton, Mass., 1948). Alan Clive, "Women Workers in World War II: Michigan as a Test Case," *Labor History,* 20 (1979) is also helpful. On the same subject, see as well Marc Miller, "Working Women and World War II," *New England Quarterly,* 53 (1980); Karen Beck Skold, "The Job He Left Behind: American Women in the Shipyards during World War II," in Carol R. Berkin and Clara M. Lovett, eds., *Women, War and Revolution* (New York, 1980); and Paddy Quick, "Rosie the Riveter: Myths and Realities," *Radical America,* 9 (1975).

Three broader treatments that provide perspective about women during the war are Alice Kessler-Harris, *Out to Work: A History of Wage-Earning Women in the United States* (New York, 1982); Carl N. Degler, *At Odds: Women and the Family in America from the Revolution to the Present* (New York, 1980); and Peter Gabriel Filene, *Him/Her/Self: Sex Roles in Modern America* (New York, 1974).

The role of blacks during World War II has also received a

good deal of attention. Neil A. Wynn, *The Afro-American and the Second World War* (New York, 1976) provides a comprehensive overview and is the place to start. Richard M. Dalfiume's article, "The Forgotten Years of the Negro Revolution," *Journal of American History,* 55 (1968) is still essential, and his book, *Desegregation of the United States Armed Forces: Fighting on Two Fronts, 1939–1953* (Columbia, Mo., 1969) is important on the military question. Another important book on the military aspect is Ulysses Lee, *The Employment of Negro Troops* (Washington, D.C., 1966). Other useful studies include: Lee Finkle, *Forum for Protest: The Black Press During World War II* (Rutherford, N.J., 1975); *John Kirby, Black Americans in the Roosevelt Era: Liberalism and Race* (Knoxville, Tenn., 1980); and August Meier and Elliott Rudwick, *CORE: A Study in the Civil Rights Movement, 1942–1968* (New York, 1973). For a more contemporary view, see Rayford W. Logan, ed., *What the Negro Wants* (Chapel Hill, N.C., 1944), and Robert Weaver, *Negro Labor* (New York, 1946).

For the difficulties of the Fair Employment Practices Committee, helpful works are: Louis Ruchames, *Race, Jobs and Politics: The Story of FEPC* (Chapel Hill, N.C., 1948); Louis C. Kesselman, *The Social Politics of FEPC* (Chapel Hill, N.C., 1948); Will Maslow, "FEPC—A Case History in Parliamentary Maneuver," *University of Chicago Law Review,* XIII (1946); and Allan M. Winkler, "The Philadelphia Transit Strike of 1944," *Journal of American History,* LIX (1972).

Wartime racial violence has come under close scrutiny. Works on the riot in Detroit include: Robert Shogan and Tom Craig, *The Detroit Race Riot: A Study in Violence* (Philadelphia, 1964); Alfred McClung Lee and Norman D. Humphrey, *Race Riot* (New York, 1943); and Harvard Sitkoff, "The Detroit Race Riot of 1943," *Michigan History,* LIII (1969). For a treatment of the Harlem uprising, see Dominic J. Capeci, *The Harlem Riot of 1943* (Philadelphia, 1977).

A number of biographical and autobiographical treatments of major black figures give a fuller sense of the struggle for civil rights. See in particular Jervis Anderson, *A. Philip Randolph: A Biographical Portrait* (New York, 1973), and Walter White, *A Rising Wind* (Garden City, N.Y., 1945).

The literature on Hispanics is less voluminous. On Mexican Americans, see Robert C. Jones, *Mexican War Workers in the United States* (Washington, D.C., 1945), Carey McWilliams, *North from Mexico: The Spanish Speaking People of the United States* (Philadelphia, 1949), and Stanley Steiner, *La Raza: The Mexican Americans* (New York, 1970). A more recent overview, Rodolfo Acuña, *Occupied America: A History of Chicanos* (New York, 1981), is also useful.

On native Americans in the war, the literature is similarly sparse. John Collier, "The Indian in a Wartime Nation," *The Annals of the American Academy of Political and Social Science,* 223 (1942) is a starting point. Alvin M. Josephy, Jr., *Now That the Buffalo's Gone: A Study of Today's Indians* (New York, 1982) describes in detail Indian struggles over the past several decades and provides a useful perspective.

For the Italian-American experience, see John P. Diggins, *Mussolini and Fascism: The View from America* (Princeton, N.J., 1972); Rudolf J. Vecoli, "The Coming of Age of the Italian Americans, 1945–1974," *Ethnicity,* 5 (1978); and Lawrence F. Pisani, *The Italian in America: A Social Study and History* (New York, 1957). Blum, *V Was for Victory,* has a useful section on wartime difficulties.

There has been a more searching examination of the Japanese-American experience during the war. Among the most useful accounts are Roger Daniels, *Concentration Camps U.S.A.: Japanese Americans and World War II* (New York, 1971); Morton Grodzins, *Americans Betrayed: Politics and the Japanese Evacuation* (Chicago, 1949); Jacobus ten Broek, Edward N. Barnhart, and Floyd W. Matson, *Prejudice, War and the Constitution* (Berkeley, California, 1954); and Audrie Girdner and Anne Loftis, *The Great Betrayal* (London, 1969). See also Bill Hosokawa, *Nisei: The Quiet Americans* (New York, 1969), and Michi Weglyn, *Years of Infamy: The Untold Story of America's Concentra-*

tion Camps (New York, 1976). For the court cases, Peter Irons, *Justice At War* (New York, 1983) is the best source.

There is a good deal of literature on the politics of the Second World War. John W. Jeffries, *Testing the Roosevelt Coalition: Connecticut Society and Politics in the Era of World War II* (Knoxville, Tenn., 1979) is an outstanding state study that goes beyond the Connecticut borders to give a full sense of the political issues of the war. On the Roosevelt coalition itself, see Samuel Lubell, *The Future of American Politics* (New York, 1951). For the growing opposition to Roosevelt that culminated in the formation of a conservative coalition, see James T. Patterson, *Congressional Conservatism and the New Deal: The Growth of the Conservative Coalition in Congress, 1933–1939* (Lexington, Ky., 1967).

For the impact of that coalition in Congress, Roland Young, *Congressional Politics in the Second World War* (New York, 1956) is still helpful. Even more pertinent and substantive is Richard N. Chapman, *Contours of Public Policy, 1939–1945* (New York, 1981). See also John Robert Moore, "The Conservative Coalition in the United States Senate, 1942–1945," *Journal of Southern History*, XXXIII (1967), and Donald R. McCoy, "Republican Opposition in Wartime, 1941–1945," *Mid-America*, XLIX (1967). John A. Salmond, *The Civilian Conservation Corps, 1933–1942* (Durham, N.C., 1967) describes the fate of one New Deal agency during the war.

For Roosevelt's efforts in connection with the GI Bill, Keith Olson, *The G.I. Bill, the Veterans, and the Colleges* (Lexington, Ky., 1974), and David R. B. Ross, *Preparing for Ulysses, 1940–1946* (New York, 1969) are both useful.

Studies focusing on important individuals provide a fuller sense of political dynamics. On the Republican side, a number of the more helpful ones include: Joseph Barnes, *Willkie* (New York, 1952); Donald Bruce Johnson, *The Republican Party and Wendell Willkie* (Urbana, Ill., 1960); Barry Keith Beyer, "Thomas E. Dewey, 1933–1947," (Ph.D. dissertation, University of Rochester, 1962); and James T. Patterson, *Mr. Republican: A Biography of Robert A. Taft* (Boston, 1972). Similar works relating to Democrats are Russell Lord, *The Wallaces of Iowa* (Boston, 1947); Norman Markowitz, *The Rise and Fall of the People's Century: Henry A. Wallace and American Liberalism, 1941–1948* (New York, 1973); John Morton Blum, ed., *The Price of Vision: The Diary of Henry A. Wallace, 1942–1946* (Boston, 1973); and Robert E. Sherwood, *Roosevelt and Hopkins* (New York, 1948). On Roosevelt himself in political campaigns, Burns, *Roosevelt: The Soldier of Freedom* contains a good deal of pertinent material. For Truman, see Cabell Phillips, *The Truman Presidency: The History of a Triumphant Succession* (New York, 1966), and Robert J. Donovan, *Conflict and Crisis: The Presidency of Harry S Truman, 1945–1948* (New York, 1977) to begin further examination.

On the question of the growth of presidential power, Richard Polenberg, *Reorganizing Roosevelt's Government:.The Controversy over Executive Reorganization, 1936–1939* (Cambridge, Mass., 1966) provides necessary background on the question of the establishment of the Executive Office. Arthur M. Schlesinger, Jr., *The Imperial Presidency* (Boston, 1973) is the essential treatment of the expansion of executive authority, both during the war and at other times.

To pursue more fully the debate over change versus continuity during World War II, see in particular the introduction in Clive, *State of War* and the last chapter in Jeffries, *Testing the Roosevelt Coalition*. Among the scholars who have documented substantial change are Polenberg, in *War and Society;* Perrett, in *Days of Sadness, Years of Triumph;* and Burns, in *Roosevelt: The Soldier of Freedom*. John Morton Blum observes the important continuities in *V Was for Victory*. Jeffries argues even more aggressively for the survival of the patterns of the past in his book and in a paper presented at the 1983 meeting of the Organization of American Historians.

INDEX

Home Front U.S.A.: America during World War II was copyedited and proofread by Elizabeth Rubenstein. Production editor was B. W. Barrett. The index was compiled by Schroeder Editorial Services. The book was typeset by Graphic Composition, Inc. and printed and bound by McNaughton & Gunn, Inc.